RADIOACTIVE DREAMS

THE CINEMA OF ALBERT PYUN

By
Justin Decloux

Radioactive Dreams: The Cinema of Albert Pyun © 2019
Written by Justin Decloux
Cover Art by Andrew Barr
Back Cover Poster Art by Keenan Marr Tamblyn
Additional Art by Duncan Bruce
Layout by Emily Milling

"WHENEVER I HAVE A HARD TIME DURING A SHOOT, I THINK BACK TO BEING A KID WORKING IN A HONOLULU GAS STATION IN THE MIDDLE OF NOWHERE. I REMEMBER DOODLING PICTURES OF MOVIE SETS AND WONDERING HOW I WAS GOING TO LEAVE THAT GODFORSAKEN INDUSTRIAL AREA TO MAKE FEATURE FILMS IN HOLLYWOOD. WELL, THE JOURNEY MAY NOT NECESSARILY BE SMOOTH, BUT IT CAN BE DONE."

- Albert Pyun

TABLE OF CONTENTS

INTRODUCTION.. 8

WHERE TO START.. 10

A NOTE ON CHRONOLOGY... 11

1: THE DAREDEVIL PERIOD

    THE SWORD AND THE SORCERER (1982)..................... 13
    RADIOACTIVE DREAMS (1985)... 17
    VICIOUS LIPS (1986)... 20

WHO IS BRICK BARDO?... 22

2: THE CANNON PERIOD

    DANGEROUSLY CLOSE (1986).. 24
    DOWN TWISTED (1987)... 27
    ALIEN FROM L.A. (1988).. 30
    JOURNEY TO THE CENTER OF THE EARTH (1988)...... 32
    CYBORG (1989)... 33
    DECEIT (1990)... 36
    CAPTAIN AMERICA (1990)... 39

NORBERT WEISSER INTERVIEW................................... 42

3: THE GOLDEN PERIOD

    KICKBOXER 2: THE ROAD BACK (1990)........................ 51
    BLOODMATCH (1991).. 54
    DOLLMAN (1991).. 56
    ARCADE (1991).. 58
    NEMESIS (1992)... 60
    KNIGHTS (1993)... 62
    BRAINSMASHER (1993)... 64
    KICKBOXER 4: THE AGGRESSOR (1994)....................... 67
    HONG KONG '97 (1994)... 69
    SPITFIRE (1995)... 71
    HEATSEEKER (1995).. 73
    NEMESIS 2: NEBULA (1995).. 75

THE DIRECTOR'S CUTS... 77

4: THE RESPECTABLE PERIOD

    NEMESIS 3: TIME LAPSE (1996) 80
    ADRENALIN: FEAR THE RUSH (1996) 82
    NEMESIS 4: DEATH ANGEL (1996) 84
    OMEGA DOOM (1996) 86
    RAVEN HAWK (1996) 88
    MEAN GUNS (1997) 90
    BLAST (1997) 92
    CRAZY SIX (1997) 94
    POSTMORTEM (1997) 96

GEORGE MOORADIAN INTERVIEW 98

5: THE WILDERNESS PERIOD

    URBAN MENACE (1999) 120
    CORRUPT (1999) 123
    THE WRECKING CREW (2000) 125
    TICKER (2001) 127
    BAD BIZNESS (2003) 129
    MAX HAVOC (2004) 131

PYUN MISCELLANEA 134

6: THE FREEDOM PERIOD

    INVASION (2005) 140
    COOL AIR (2006) 142
    LEFT FOR DEAD (2007) 144
    ROAD TO HELL (2008) 146
    BULLETFACE (2010) 148
    ABELAR: TALES OF AN ANCIENT EMPIRE (2010) 152
    SLINGER (1989/2013) 154
    THE INTERROGATION OF CHERYL COOPER (2014) 156

TONY RIPARETTI INTERVIEW 158

THE PYUN PLAYERS 168

EPILOGUE 170

BIBLIOGRAPHY 174

SPECIAL THANKS 175

WHY HASN'T ANYONE EVER WRITTEN A BOOK ON ALBERT PYUN?

The man's got one hell of an origin story: He came out of Hawaii without any industry contacts, fought hard in Hollywood to get his vision to the screen, and somehow hit box office gold the first time out the gate. He made movies for a failing studio, directed one of the most reviled superhero films of all times, and built a creative family who worked fast, cheap and prolifically. Most of his pictures went direct to video, but it didn't matter to him and his team, because they tackled every project like it would be shown on the biggest screen in the world.

Most people don't hold a very high opinion of Albert Pyun's output. His films received negative reviews when they were released, and he was called an opportunist, a hack, and a no-talent filmmaker. His most well-known accomplishment was directing the primo slice of 80s cheese that is Jean-Claude Van Damme's CYBORG (1989).

My fascination with Albert Pyun began when I saw NEMESIS (1992). I was blown away by Pyun's wildly energetic film making style and his take on John Woo action mixed in with a goofy cyberpunk aesthetic. And the more I read about this career, the more interested I became. I discovered that Pyun made a film in secret while shooting pickups for CYBORG, that he often filmed scenes on busy streets without permits to get the perfect shot and that he always worked with the same actors and technical team because he liked a familial vibe on set. To me, Pyun didn't sound like a hack at all. He sounded like a driven filmmaker who fought tooth and nail for every project.

Even if you're not a big fan of his output, it's undeniable that his career has it all: Ambition, success, drama, failure, a fiery need to create, a lot more failure, and a jaw-dropping amount of persevering.

There were so many times in Albert Pyun's career where it would have made perfect sense to throw in the towel, but he never did, because making movies was his everything. Pyun started to work in the film industry in 1982, and in 2005 when the money dried up, and the investors stopped returning his calls, he even began to pay for his productions out of pocket.

That's why I had to write a book about him.

I knew I was never going to be able to put together the definitive text on Albert Pyun. Instead, my modest goal was to watch all of his available movies and compose a few critical thoughts on them. I want to share Pyun's journey, his passion and the cinematic gems I discovered along the way. My main hope with this project is that it will make people raise an eyebrow and say, "A book about the director of CYBORG? What could there possibly be to say about him?"

AND THEN THEY FIND OUT

WHERE TO START

THE PYUN ESSENTIALS

My favourite Albert Pyun films.

- NEMESIS
- RADIOACTIVE DREAMS
- DECEIT
- MEAN GUNS
- SLINGER (The Director's Cut of CYBORG)

PURE ENTERTAINMENT PYUN

Turn off your brain and enjoy.

- BRAINSMASHER…A LOVE STORY
- KNIGHTS
- SPITFIRE
- SWORD AND THE SORCERER
- KICKBOXER 2: THE ROAD BACK

UNDERRATED PYUN

They deserve a second chance.

- NEMESIS 2: NEBULA
- BLAST
- CAPTAIN AMERICA
- ADRENALIN: FEAR THE RUSH
- LEFT FOR DEAD

EXPERIMENTAL PYUN

For the adventurous at heart.

- VICIOUS LIPS
- INVASION
- NEMESIS 4: DEATH ANGEL
- CRAZY SIX
- POSTMORTEM

A NOTE ON CHRONOLOGY

I've done my best to present the films in shooting order instead of release order to better reflect Pyun's evolution as a filmmaker. It's not an exact science due to a lack of documentation, so please excuse any incorrect dates.

RELEASE ORDER

THE SWORD AND THE SORCERER (1982)
RADIOACTIVE DREAMS (1985)
DANGEROUSLY CLOSE (1986)
VICIOUS LIPS (1986)
DOWN TWISTED (1987)
ALIEN FROM L.A. (1988)
JOURNEY TO THE CENTER OF THE EARTH (1988)
CYBORG (1989)
DECEIT (1990)
CAPTAIN AMERICA (1990)
KICKBOXER 2: THE ROAD BACK (1991)
BLOODMATCH (1991)
DOLLMAN (1991)
NEMESIS (1992)
KNIGHTS (1993)
BRAINSMASHER (1993)
ARCADE (1993)
KICKBOXER 4: THE AGGRESSOR (1994)
HONG KONG '97 (1994)
SPITFIRE (1995)
NEMESIS 2: NEBULA (1995)
HEATSEEKER (1995)
ADRENALIN: FEAR THE RUSH (1996)
NEMESIS 3: TIME LAPSE (1996)
RAVEN HAWK (1996)
OMEGA DOOM (1996)
NEMESIS 4: DEATH ANGEL (1996)
BLAST (1997)
MEAN GUNS (1997)
CRAZY SIX (1997)
POSTMORTEM (1997)
URBAN MENACE (1999)
CORRUPT (1999)
THE WRECKING CREW (2000)
TICKER (2001)
BAD BIZNESS (2003)
MAX HAVOC (2004)
INVASION (2005)
COOL AIR (2006)
LEFT FOR DEAD (2007)
ROAD TO HELL (2008)
BULLETFACE (2010)
ABELAR: TALES OF AN ANCIENT EMPIRE (2010)
THE INTERROGATION OF CHERYL COOPER (2014)

SHOOTING ORDER

THE SWORD AND THE SORCERER (1982)
RADIOACTIVE DREAMS (1985)
VICIOUS LIPS (1986)
DANGEROUSLY CLOSE (1986)
DOWN TWISTED (1987)
ALIEN FROM L.A. (1988)
JOURNEY TO THE CENTER OF THE EARTH (1988)
CYBORG (1989)
DECEIT (1990)
CAPTAIN AMERICA (1990)
KICKBOXER 2 (1991)
BLOODMATCH (1991)
DOLLMAN (1991)
ARCADE (1991)
NEMESIS (1992)
KNIGHTS (1993)
BRAINSMASHER (1993)
KICKBOXER 4: THE AGGRESSOR (1994)
HONG KONG '97 (1994)
SPITFIRE (1995)
HEATSEEKER (1995)
NEMESIS 2: NEBULA (1995)
NEMESIS 3: TIME LAPSE (1996)
ADRENALIN: FEAR THE RUSH (1996)
NEMESIS 4: DEATH ANGEL (1996)
OMEGA DOOM (1996)
RAVEN HAWK (1996)
MEAN GUNS (1997)
BLAST (1997)
CRAZY SIX (1997)
POSTMORTEM (1997)
URBAN MENACE (1999)
CORRUPT (1999)
THE WRECKING CREW (2000)
TICKER (2001)
BAD BIZNESS (2003)
MAX HAVOC (2004)
INVASION (2005)
COOL AIR (2006)
LEFT FOR DEAD (2007)
ROAD TO HELL (2008)
BULLETFACE (2010)
ABELAR: TALES OF AN ANCIENT EMPIRE (2010)
THE INTERROGATION OF CHERYL COOPER (2014)

THE DAREDEVIL PERIOD

SWORD AND THE SORCERER (1982) - VICIOUS LIPS (1986)

This period begins with Pyun's break into the industry with THE SWORD AND THE SORCERER and follows through the disastrous productions of RADIOACTIVE DREAMS and VICIOUS LIPS. The three films in this cycle are all notable for being high concept ideas that were incredibly difficult to pull off.

THE SWORD AND THE SORCERER (1982)

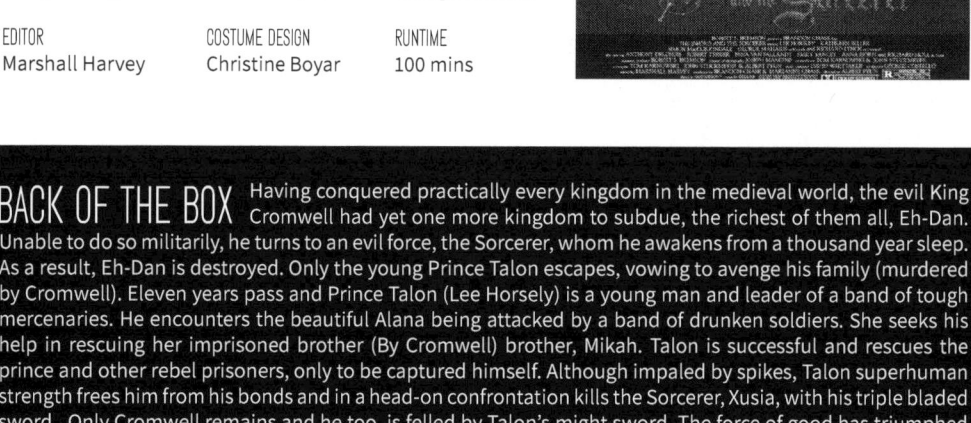

CAST
Lee Horsley, Kathleen Beller, Simon MacCorkindale

WRITERS
Tom Karnowski, John Stuckmeyer, Albert Pyun

PRODUCERS
Marianne Chase, Brandon Chase, Mark L. Rosen

CINEMATOGRAPHER
Joseph Mangine

MUSIC
David Whitaker

ART DIRECTION
George Costello

EDITOR
Marshall Harvey

COSTUME DESIGN
Christine Boyar

RUNTIME
100 mins

BACK OF THE BOX Having conquered practically every kingdom in the medieval world, the evil King Cromwell had yet one more kingdom to subdue, the richest of them all, Eh-Dan. Unable to do so militarily, he turns to an evil force, the Sorcerer, whom he awakens from a thousand year sleep. As a result, Eh-Dan is destroyed. Only the young Prince Talon escapes, vowing to avenge his family (murdered by Cromwell). Eleven years pass and Prince Talon (Lee Horsely) is a young man and leader of a band of tough mercenaries. He encounters the beautiful Alana being attacked by a band of drunken soldiers. She seeks his help in rescuing her imprisoned brother (By Cromwell) brother, Mikah. Talon is successful and rescues the prince and other rebel prisoners, only to be captured himself. Although impaled by spikes, Talon superhuman strength frees him from his bonds and in a head-on confrontation kills the Sorcerer, Xusia, with his triple bladed sword. Only Cromwell remains and he too, is felled by Talon's might sword. The force of good has triumphed over the forces of evil!

THE SWORD AND THE SORCERER is every straight teenage boy's fantasy: A rollicking epic featuring a swashbuckling hero, dastardly villains, and an insane amount of naked women. It's sobering to consider that at the time of its release, no one was making films like it — but that didn't stop a 28-year-old Hawaiian hopeful named Albert Pyun and his two friends Tom Karnowski and John V. Stuckmeyer from going to Hollywood to get it made.

They didn't have any credits to their name, but they had a script and storyboards, and naively assumed their enthusiasm would get them the gig. It did not. Every door was slammed in their face. No one wanted the silly fantasy stuff. They wanted STAR WARS style science-fiction blockbusters! It wasn't until John Boorman's EXCALIBUR (1981) became a box-office bonanza that the money-men changed their tune. Suddenly, every producer needed a sword and sorcery project and CONAN: THE BARBARIAN, DEATHSTALKER and THE BEASTMASTER all served an audience hungry for a genre that hadn't been exploited since the Italian Sword and Sandal Peplums.

Barry Chase was the producer that brought THE SWORD AND THE SORCERER to the screen. He had already turned down Pyun and his friends once, but the success of EXCALIBUR made the project viable, so he jumped on the chance to procure a ready-made property that was entirely storyboarded! Albert Pyun was given the go-ahead to direct, but he was just a kid, so Barry felt he could push him around. The producer had directed three soft-core sex films. He knew how this stuff worked.

Right from the start, Pyun couldn't catch a break. From all accounts, his experience on SWORD was a miserable one. No one had any faith in his abilities. Lee Horsley was cast as the hero Talon against Albert's wishes. Oliver Reed was supposed to do the narration, but he showed up to the recording session insanely drunk. Barry Chase shot extra violence without Albert's consent to compete with the R-rating of CONAN: THE BARBARIAN. It was a nightmare situation; A novice filmmaker in charge of an insanely complicated project with a producer that had no qualms steamrolling over him to get to the finish line.

With that in mind, It's a miracle SWORD is as fun as it is. It's got Pyun's out-there ideas, his careful framing, and a 30-minute prologue that takes place over decades and tells the story of kingdoms won, lost and recaptured. It's a device common in fantasy novels but rarely executed on screen. We don't meet the adult Talon (Lee Horsley) until a half-hour into the picture! And even then, he's only one piece of the puzzle. There's also the treacherous warlord Cromwell (a deliciously evil Richard Lynch) who wants to marry the princess (Kathleen Baler) to take over the kingdom. And of course, a gang of friendly mercenaries, some rival clans, a prostitute with a heart of gold, and a melting sorcerer (Richard Mogg) who is resurrected, killed and revived again within the first twenty minutes.

It's undeniable that from a storytelling perspective, SWORD is one shaky package. It plays out in fits and starts, has difficulty juggling its many characters, and unfortunately leans into the sexist tropes of the genre. None of this bothered its target audience. They were just happy to see all the stuff that had been trapped in the yellowed pages of the novels of Michael Moorcock on screen! And oh boy, did SWORD deliver. There are long

fights through castles... crawls through torch-lit sewers infested with flesh-eating rats... so many naked women... Gory violence. Evil monsters. Heroic crucifixions. Lee Horsey is incredibly charming as Talon. The action is clunky but ferocious. Richard Lynch chews the scenery. The practical effects are a joy to watch in all their wobbly glory. The smoky soft-focus cinematography is reminiscent of

Boorman's EXCALIBUR, but it's got textural grit, and while the film may be a narrative mess, it also feels like there's a world that exists beyond the frame. Pyun didn't look down on the material like his producer. He genuinely loved it! SWORD isn't a gentle bore like fantasy films along the line of KRULL. Its pure unapologetic pulp executed with vigour and passion. The SWORD AND THE SORCERER also features one of the most absurd weapons in film history: A large broadsword that can shoot out its three blades at rocket powered speeds. It's laughably impracticable and amazing to see portrayed on screen without a hint of condescension.

In the end, the film was completed, the production commissioned an amazing painted poster by Peter Andrew Jones, and THE SWORD AND THE SORCERER became a shockingly big box office hit (It cost $4 million and grossed $40 million). Sadly, the first credit on screen is A BARRY CHASE FILM. The picture's success did nothing for Albert's career. He wouldn't direct another feature for three years.

I can't imagine being in Pyun's shoes after SWORD AND THE SORCERER was released. Finally, his dream of being a filmmaker had come true. The box-office results proved to him the world liked what he had to offer. Yet, the film had been taken out of his hands and changed against his wishes, he had been marginalized throughout the production, and the critics labelled the movie as trash.

He could have given up right there, and no one would have faulted him for it.

But he didn't.

HE WAS A FILMMAKER AFTER ALL.

FUN FACT An anecdote that pops up all the time is that Albert Pyun was mentored by Akira Kurosawa. It's a great bit of myth making, but it's not quite the whole truth. What really happened was that Albert was asked to intern on Kurosawa's film DERSU UZULA (1975) by Japanese mega star Toshiro Mifune (They bonded over one of Pyun's short films), but when Mifune dropped out of Kurosawa's film, Albert ended up working with the star on a number of Japanese TV shows instead. Pyun said the experience was incredibly insightful and that he learned a lot from Kurosawa's cinematographer Takao Saito

RADIOACTIVE DREAMS (1985)

CAST
John Stockwell, Michael Dudikoff, Michele Little

WRITERS
Albert Pyun

PRODUCERS
Moctesuma Esparza, Tom Karnowski

CINEMATOGRAPHER
Charles Minsky

MUSIC
Peter Manning Robinson

ART DIRECTION
Chester Kaczenski

EDITOR
Dennis M. O'Connor

COSTUME DESIGN
Christine Boyar

RUNTIME
98 min

BACK OF THE BOX John Stockwell (CHRISTINE, CITY LIMITS), Lisa Blount (AN OFFICER AND A GENTLEMAN), Michael Dudikoff (BACHELOR PARTY) and screen veteran George Kennedy stars in this far out comic fantasy film RADIOACTIVE DREAMS.

RADIOACTIVE DREAMS is a goofy '80s comedy, a post-apocalyptic adventure, a '40s detective pastiche, and a musical all wrapped into one high-concept package. Albert Pyun sure didn't take the easy road.

On the day the nuclear bombs drop, two boys are stuffed in a bunker by their fathers and abandoned. They're stuck in the underground prison with only pulp detective novels to keep them company. By the time they find a way out they've grown into two adults who dream of being private eyes and now go by the names Phillip Chandler (Future KICKBOXER: VENGEANCE director John Stockwell) and Marlowe Hammer (Mr. AMERICAN NINJA himself - Michael Dudikoff). They head out into the wasteland with nothing but a slick car, nice suits, and the hope that they'll stumble on some juicy mysteries. What's the worst that could happen to two clueless detectives running head-on into an irradiated world populated with murderous mutants?

RADIOACTIVE DREAMS is a blast of a motion picture — at once silly and surprisingly emotional. As the more excited of the two leads, Dudikoff is excellent in a comedic role that asks him to act with childlike glee. Stockwell gets to be the more serious one, but that's only so he can do the hard-boiled narration. The supporting cast includes a gang of red-headed bikers, a giant killer rat, two foul-mouthed kid assassins and a spy looking for nuclear launch codes (Lisa Blount). And last but not least there's the third star of the picture: An amazing fourteen-song soundtrack made up of bands fronted by women vocalists. The picture only drops the ball on the promise of being a road movie, because by the end of the first act, the story heads into an underground city and never escapes. At least Pyun and cinematographer Charles Minski make the neon lit industrial sets pop off the screen in bold colours.

If the shooting of SWORD AND THE SORCERER was a nightmare, then RADIOACTIVE DREAMS was hell. It was a complicated project that involved the desert, special effects, stunts, and musical numbers, but I don't think Pyun ever thought the worst could happen; That a bond company would take over the film. Most productions take out an insurance policy to guarantee that if something terrible happens during the shoot, and the project looks unfinishable, a bond company representative will wrap things up. If the bond company steps in, it's a death sentence to anyone creatively invested in a project. In this case, the budget dried up at some point, and the hatchet men were sent in to complete the picture.

I don't know what Pyun shot and what was done by an anonymous stooge, but it's pretty clear that some scenes suffer from a "Just get it done" execution. After an enthusiastic opening, the rapid-fire pace grinds to a halt. For a film about the post-apocalypse, it sure gets pretty cramped and claustrophobic as the story of two naive men looking for adventure hits a dead end.

The picture strips away the fun of its premise and forces Phillip and Marlowe to experience the rigours of harsh reality. They lose their fancy suits, get betrayed by everyone they meet, and learn that life isn't a straightforward romp. But in their toughening up, they both realize that they had the right-attitude from the get-go: You gotta stay positive no matter how bad it gets. If you give in to the misery of the world, you'll always be lost. So, why not dance instead?

I was worried that the characters quest to find their fathers would lead to a "Chosen One" style reveal, but the film pulls the brilliant move of giving them an opaque answer to

their origins: "What's the difference? The past is the past. Get on with your life, kid." Even this early in his career, Pyun was already undercutting genre expectations.

RADIOACTIVE DREAMS has been forgotten over the years, and it's a real shame. It's undeniably flawed, but what isn't? I've seen the film on 35mm, and it's a colourful ride that the faded DVD and VHS releases don't adequately capture.

Let's get it out in high definition!

FUN FACT The most prominent band on the soundtrack with four numbers is Sue Saad and the Next. Albert liked them so much he even included Sue Saad in the film singing one of her songs and the relationship with the band continued when he asked Jim Saad and Tony Riparetti to compose the soundtracks for some of his movies. Tony would eventually go solo and score a whopping 32 of Albert's projects.

DOUBLE FUN FACT Around this time, Pyun was hired to direct a very early version of TOTAL RECALL with William Hurt in the lead role, but the studio lost interest and pulled the plug. Pyun has said his version was nothing like the big action movie Paul Verhoeven ended up making with Arnold Schwarzenegger

VICIOUS LIPS (1986)

CAST
Dru-Anne Perry, Gina Calabrese, Linda Kerridge

WRITER
Albert Pyun

PRODUCERS
Tom Karnowski

CINEMATOGRAPHER
Tim Suhrstedt

MUSIC
Michael McCarty

PRODUCTION DESIGN
Bob Ziembicki

EDITOR
Rozanne Zingale

COSTUME DESIGN
Sarah Bardo

RUNTIME
84 mins

BACK OF THE BOX A band finally gets the opportunity for that breakthrough gig if they can make it to an "in" club on another planet in time.

THE POSTER of VICIOUS LIPS promises the intergalactic adventures of an all-women rock 'n' roll band. The final result is a disorienting half-finished nightmare. It's got a great premise: The up-and-coming musicians "The Vicious Lips" must race across the universe to make it to their first big gig, but instead of going on a goofy galactic road trip, their spaceship instantly crash lands on a desert planet, and we spend the rest of the film watching the unenthused band members — who can only be told apart by their wigs — walk through nondescript hallways. There's an escaped monster on the loose who looks like a half-transformed werewolf, but he doesn't do diddly squat! The film devolves into a head-scratching finale where the lead singer runs through a haunted house populated by cannibals, and it's all revealed to be nothing but a dream. The running time is padded out with the band singing "Lunar Madness" over TWO montages of scenes we just witnessed. Ouch. On the plus side, the film looks great thanks to the colourful cinematography of Tim Suhrstedt, and we do get some catchy 80's-style power synth songs by Sue Saad and The Next.

I hated VICIOUS LIPS the first time I saw it, but on this viewing, it revealed itself as an Antonioni-esque tale of stasis, with the dreamy feel of a cut-rate LAST YEAR AT MARIENBAD (1961). It's impossible for me to watch the film and not wonder if Pyun was unconsciously articulating his own state of mind. VICIOUS LIPS was supposed to be Pyun's 'prove them wrong' follow-up to SWORD and RADIOACTIVE DREAMS; A simple, high concept, saleable product that could be knocked out quickly in seven days to the tune of $100,000. It obviously wasn't enough time or money, because the picture stinks of sheer desperation. Master shots are edited haphazardly together in a dreamy style,

subplots are introduced and dropped, and whole conversations are steamrolled into musical montages. Yet, the bareness of its visual style and uneventful story seem to be a door into Pyun's emotional state: The lead singer, desperately wants to be a star and is willing to do anything to achieve it, and all she gets for her troubles is misery. Just like Pyun always seemed to be on the cusp of Hollywood success, before being tossed back into the no-budget ghetto. It may seem like a simple in-joke that The Vicious Lips are going to get their big break at The Radioactive Dream, but it's way sadder when you consider what that means in the context of Pyun's career. I don't think its a coincidence that the title song of the film is called "Reach for you Dreams" and the chorus goes "You gotta reach for your dream! Don't let it slip away! Nothing can hold you back this time."

Empire Picture pictures released VICIOUS LIPS quietly in a few theatres and dumped it on video in a handful of countries that did not include North America or the UK. It was missing for years on a digital format until it was released on Blu-ray by Shout Factory in 2017.

WHO IS
BRICK BARDO?

The character name Brick Bardo appears nine times in Pyun's filmography. The moniker was first used in RADIOACTIVE DREAMS, but it's most famous iteration is Tim Thomerson's character in DOLLMAN. Other cases include Thom Andrews's villain in BLOODMATCH, Scott Paulin's horny alien in DECEIT, and Ralf Moeller's muscle bound baddie in CYBORG.

When asked about its repeated use, Pyun has said he simply enjoyed the sound of the name because it has a late 50s, early 60s ring to it, like Tab Hunter or Rock Hudson. Brick Bardo was also the nickname of cameraman Joe Bardo, who Pyun has said was instrumental in helping him out early in his career (and who produced VICIOUS LIPS)

Joe Bardo is probably most famous for appearing in the films of mad genius Ray Dennis Steckler (THE THRILL KILLERS and LEMON GROVE KIDS MEET THE MONSTERS). Bardo also directed a few adult films under the name Lisa Barr and B.D Smith.

Pyun would often use pseudonyms on his projects because he believed there was something cheap about seeing the same name multiple time in the credits. Some of his best known aliases include Hannah Blue (Writer on BLAST) and Kitty Chalmers (Writer on CYBORG).

THE CANNON PERIOD

DANGEROUSLY CLOSE (1986) - CAPTAIN AMERICA (1990)

This period encompasses the time Pyun worked for The Cannon Film Group. His early work for the company was slick, but had a little less personality, while later titles suffered as Cannon slid into bankruptcy. The period contains his most famous film CYBORG and arguably his most reviled, CAPTAIN AMERICA.

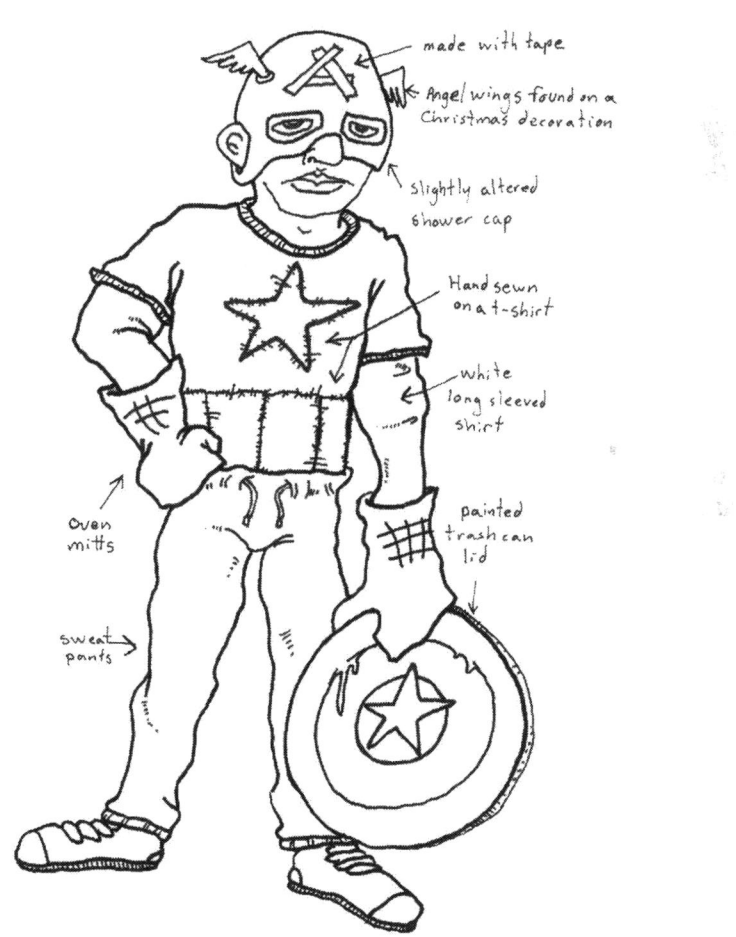

DANGEROUSLY CLOSE (1986)

CAST
John Stockwell, J. Eddie Peck, Carey Lowell

WRITERS
Scott Fields, Marty Ross, John Stockwell

PRODUCER
Harold Sobel

CINEMATOGRAPHER
Walt Lloyd

MUSIC
Michael McCarty

PRODUCTION DESIGNER
Marcia Hinds

EDITOR
Dennis M. O'Connor

COSTUME DESIGN
Dana Sanchez

RUNTIME
95 mins

BACK OF THE BOX If you're not part of the in-crowd at this trendy upscale high school, it could mean the end of more than just your academic life...

IN DANGEROUSLY CLOSE Pyun plays it safe. After three disastrous productions, DANGEROUSLY CLOSE was his attempt to tell a simple story without any frills. He wanted to prove to producers that he wasn't just a weird experimental artist. He could tone it down and deliver palatable pop entertainment. It would also be the first time he worked for Cannon Films head-honchos Golan & Globus.

DANGEROUSLY CLOSE is an anonymous entry in the "Teenage Yuppy Jackasses" genre, even if its opening seems to indicate it'll be harder-edged, and will play like a mixture of CLASS OF 1984 and THE MOST DANGEROUS GAME. In the dead of night, a kid finds himself being chased by a bunch of masked hunters with crossbows. The kid is caught, trussed up, and just as he's begging for his life, they cut him loose and reveal its nothing but a cruel joke. Or is it? Before the title card hits, the kid's throat is slit.

Is it the High School sanctioned vigilante group The Sentinels who are responsible? Or is it one lone killer that's broken free from the pack?

Sadly, the script by co-star John Stockwell (RADIOACTIVE DREAMS actor and future BLUE CRUSH director) never commits to the exploitative premise. Things play out like an earnest made-for-TV movie about the dangers of yuppiedom than the actual "Slobs vs Snobs" action film the promotional art promises. The killer's body count adds up to only two people! And it takes ages for the film's bland working-class protagonist with

the world's bushiest eyebrows (J. Eddie Peck) to figure out that the school's rich kids are up to something, and once he does, things get wrapped up without much incident. Pyun indulges in a few weird angles and jarring cross-cuts, but for the most part, the film plays like generic MTV music video: Lots of blue light, Tony Scott smoke, and a blaring soundtrack filled with Depeche Mode. The film does mark the start of The Pyun's Players with Thom Mathews appearing in a supporting role and Don Michael Paul (who would return in ALIEN FROM L.A.) making his screen debut. The appearance of the female-fronted band Lost Pilots is also classic Pyun, but it feels like a watered down version of Sue Saad and The Next.

The one thing that genuinely surprised me was the story's big reveal: It's not the teens who had been committing the murders, but the deranged dean of their fancy high-school. His motivation is brazenly tossed off as PTSD from a tour in Vietnam, but the film is much more interested in the bullies reactions to the news: They believed they were in the right, and the revelation that they were being led by a psychotic adult, saps them of their convictions. It's a bold turn, but it means the bullies never get their just desserts or deal with any real consequences for their actions. It would have been interesting if the bullies were forced to reckon with the emotional damage their "games" have caused, but it never happens.

The film was principally a chance for Pyun to prove that he could pull something off without setting off any alarms. It was an experience that would lead to a loyal stretch with Cannon Films just as they were going bankrupt.

FUN FACT When Steven Soderbergh was looking for a cinematographer for his first film SEX, LIES AND VIDEOTAPE (1989), someone suggested he hire DANGEROUSLY CLOSE cinematographer Walt Lloyd. Soderbergh watched a tape of DANGEROUSLY CLOSE and said he didn't like the guy's style. Surprisingly, he still ended up hiring Lloyd, and they worked together on SEX, LIES and Soderbergh's underrated follow-up KAFKA (1991).

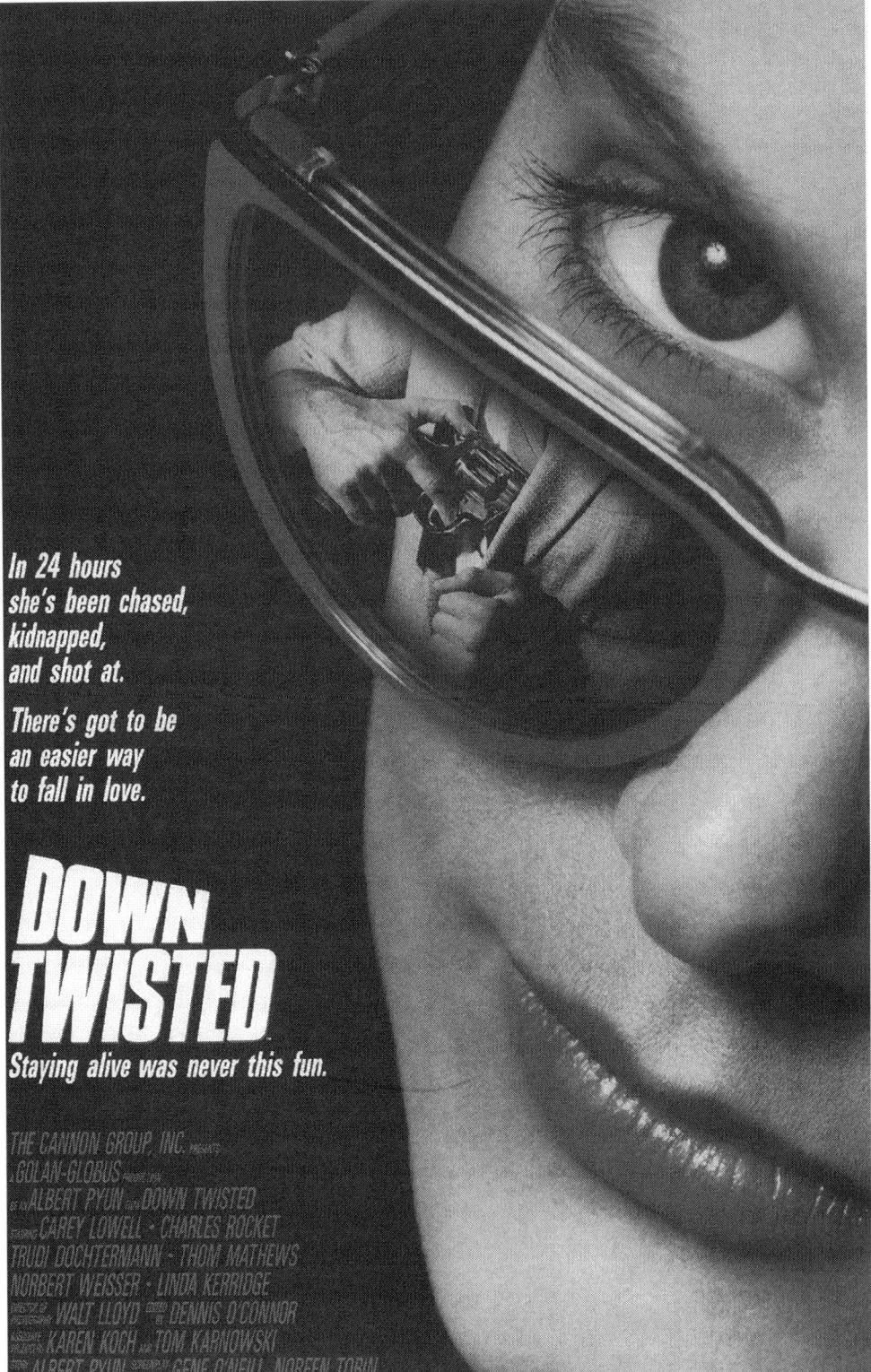

DOWN TWISTED (1987)

CAST
Carey Lowell, Charles Rocket, Trudy Dochterman

WRITERS
Gene O'Neill, Noreen Tobin

PRODUCERS
Yoram Globus, Menahem Golan

CINEMATOGRAPHER
Walt Lloyd

MUSIC
Eric Allaman

PRODUCTION DESIGNER
Chester Kaczenski

EDITOR
Dennis M. O'Connor

COSTUME DESIGN
Renee Johnston

RUNTIME
88 mins

BACK OF THE BOX Down Twisted is a who's who? Who dunnit? And who'll get away with it? Fast, gripping and often very funny, there's one thing that's certain - a big deal is going down and it's going down twisted.

SOMETIMES it'll take me a moment to get in sync with an Albert Pyun film. They may all seem similar on the surface (Cyberpunk! Muscular Women! Rock 'N' Roll!), and he often dives into the same bag of stylistic tricks (Wide angle lens! Coloured lights! Inserts!), but every project still comes with its own distinct flavour. For example, KNIGHTS (1993) may look like another try at the post-apocalyptic Spaghetti Western he tackled with CYBORG (1989), but it has more in common with the new-wave flying swordsman genre of Tsui Hark's THE BLADE (1995) than Jean-Claude doing the splits. Or you'd expect NEMESIS 2: NEBULA (1995) to be related to the Olivier Gruner original, but Pyun drew inspiration instead from THE NAKED PREY (1965). If you go into a Pyun film expecting a straight-ahead action film, there's a good chance you'll walk away disappointed, but if you go in with an open mind, there's a great chance you'll be pleasantly surprised.

DOWN TWISTED opens with a title card that says six people robbed the Crucible of San Lucas, switched it with a replica and flew the original to Los Angeles. On arrival, one of the thieves betrays the others and makes a break for it. In the middle of all of this, a young waitress (played by DANGEROUSLY CLOSE and LAW & ORDER's Carey Lowell) is picked up by her roommate, who also happens to be the girlfriend of the defecting thief. The roommate gets Cary Lowell in trouble, seemingly dies in an explosion (wink! wink!) and Lowell finds herself shipped off to San Lucas and chased by the remaining thieves because they think she has the key to the treasure. Her only hope is a sleaze-ball lawyer (played by ex-SNL member Charles Rocket) who may know more than he's letting on.

From that synopsis, you could assume DOWN TWISTED is a pulpy ROMANCING THE STONE-style pastiche. It isn't. Maybe a heist film? Nope. How about a straight-ahead globe-trotting action adventure? Still no.

So, what is it exactly?

For one, the style is much more prosaic than Pyun's previous productions. He lets the shots breathe and ditches the close-ups. In their place, he uses massive wides filled with intricate details. Every cut reveals another 'Perfect Shot' layered with areas of primary colour so rich they would make Dario Argento jealous. Once I stopped waiting for a set-piece to break out, I realized what Pyun was trying to do: He was riffing on Michael Mann's THIEF (1981).

The colours. The scope. The focus on professional criminals. It all clicked into place. Like a lot of Pyun's attempts, it can get pretty shaky at times. He grasps the surface details, but the internal mechanics grind. The characters are too goofy, Carey Lowell is not proactive enough, and the film is continuously teasing that something big is coming, but nothing ever does. Once I came to terms with the film's stylistic template, I was able to enjoy what Pyun was trying to do: A walk through a burning forest. A chase through a parade. A tense confrontation in an airport.

Is it still too slow? Probably. Was the outcome a little too on the nose? Absolutely. It doesn't help that the film obviously ran under time, so the final moments are hilariously stretched out before the end credits roll (which are fifteen minutes long!). But for all those deficiencies, there's still an accomplished air to the production that's rarely present in most of Pyun's cash-strapped endeavours. I wasn't surprised to learn that he considers this one of his favourite films because he went in with a specific idea and was able to pull it off.

ALIEN FROM L.A. (1988)

CAST
Kathy Ireland, William R. Moses, Richard Haines

WRITERS
Debra Ricci, Sandra Berg, Albert Pyun

PRODUCERS
Yoram Globus, Menahem Golan

CINEMATOGRAPHER
Tom Fraser

MUSIC
Jim Andron, Steve LeGassick, Anthony Riparetti, James Saad

PRODUCTION DESIGNER
Pamela B. Warner

EDITOR
Daniel Loewenthal

COSTUME DESIGN
Birgitta Bjerke

RUNTIME
87 mins

BACK OF THE BOX Wanda is a lonely L.A. girl living with her crazy aunt. Nothing ever happens in her life until... She discovers that her explorer-adventurer father who deserted Wanda years ago, has fallen down a bottomless pit in Africa and is presumed dead. Wanda searches for him and soon finds herself in the underground city of Atlantis full of the strangest people imaginable.

"PLEASE GOD, CAN YOU MAKE SOMETHING HAPPEN IN MY LIFE? ANYTHING AT ALL? REALLY?"
- Wanda Saknussemm (Kathy Ireland) in ALIEN FROM L.A.

ALIEN FROM L.A. is famous for one thing and one thing only: Kathy Ireland's voice. The sound that emanates from her mouth can be described as a piercing shriek, the cartoon version of a Valley Girl twang, and nails on a chalkboard all rolled into one. Albert Pyun deliberately asked her to use that voice, and it highlights his creative strengths and weaknesses in one fell swoop: There was a logical rationale behind the decision, but he forgot an audience would have to live with it for 90 minutes. The story of ALIEN FROM L.A. is a riff on ALICE IN WONDERLAND, but instead of an adventurous lass, the protagonist is a shy girl trapped in an adult's body. So, how can that be made clearer? Well, she could have a kid's voice of course! And she could never shut up! An excellent idea on paper. A brutal reality in execution.

The film doesn't know how to sell its "Kathy Ireland is a Nerd" set-up (she wears glasses, I guess?), so it covers the early soundtrack in a wall of generic '80s comedy music that only dissipates when Ireland falls down a hole and lands in Atlantis. It's in the underground that Pyun finds himself in his element. He visualizes the buried world as a post-apocalyptic landscape reminiscent of his previous film RADIOACTIVE DREAMS. There are punks as far as the eye can see, and every cramped set (well executed by production designer Pamela B. Warner) is filled with smoke. The one difference between this and RADIOACTIVE DREAMS is that Pyun's main inspiration seems to have been Terry

Gilliam's BRAZIL. The world of ALIEN FROM L.A. is made up of giant TVs that broadcast state-sponsored "news" at every turn, vehicles look like a toddler designed them, and there's even a set modelled after the interrogation room from Terry Gilliam's masterpiece that toes very close to copyright infringement territory. I was surprised to discover that Pyun didn't work with his regular collaborators on ALIEN FROM L.A. because the film was shot in Africa, which  goes to show that his cinema's garish music video style, wild make-up designs and neon-lit sets have always been pure Pyun. ALIEN FROM L.A. sports four composers, but by the halfway mark it feels like Pyun's right-hand man Tony Riparetti took over with some rocking electric guitar.

Unfortunately, ALIEN FROM L.A. never rises above the confines of being "Fine." All the signifiers of Pyun's golden period are in place, but even when Pyun shifts the costume and set design to mirror Powell and Pressburger's THIEF OF BAGHDAD (turbans!), and Thom Mathews shows up as a swashbuckling a hero called Charming, it still struggles to generate any excitement. It looks and sounds like an adventure romp, but there's not much adventuring going on, and all an audience has to focus on are Ireland's bug-eyed reactions. The film's "Face your Fears" message is clear, but the allusions to ALICE IN WONDERLAND and WIZARD OF OZ are evident to the point of annoyance, and no matter how many times characters point out that Kathy's voice is grating, it doesn't make listening to it any easier.

The presence of ALIEN FROM L.A. may look like an oddity at first in the filmography of the Cannon Film Group, the production company most famous for popularizing Chuck Norris slaughtering thousands of communists, but it's relatively consistent with the company's direction in 1988. They tried to diversify into a more mainstream path with mega-flops like SUPERMAN: QUEST FOR PEACE. The production of ALIEN FROM L.A. was simply another stab at the Family Adventure format. For all of its provocative poster art of Ireland in a low-cut top and ripped jeans, her character is never portrayed as anything other than innocently childlike (without ever toeing into Lolita territory). Her utterances of slang words like "Bitchin" serve the purpose of a kid-like "Gee Whiz", and the film never forces her to "toughen up" or use her sexuality in any outward way. She's simply a woman who goes on an adventure.

FUN FACT The boyfriend that dumps Ireland in the opening is played by Don Michael Paul, who would later go on to direct Steven Seagal's last theatrical film as a star, HALF-PAST DEAD (2002). Don Michael Paul currently has a career directing DTV films like TREMORS: A COLD DAY IN HELL (the sixth one!) and THE SCORPION KING: BOOK OF POWER (the fifth one!). I bet he learned a lot working with Albert

JOURNEY TO THE CENTER OF THE EARTH (1988)

DIRECTOR
Rusty Lemorande (Uncredited - Albert Pyun)

CAST
Nicola Cowper, Ilan Mitchell-Smith, Paul Carafotes

WRITERS
Debra Ricci, Sandra Berg, Albert Pyun, Rusty Lemorande

PRODUCER
Yoram Globus, Menahem Golan

CINEMATOGRAPHER
Tom Fraser, David Watkin

MUSIC
(Uncredited)

COSTUME DESIGN
Birgitta Bjerke, Betty Pecha Madden

PRODUCTION DESIGNER
Geoffrey Kirkland

RUNTIME
100 mins

BACK OF THE BOX Exploring a mysterious cavern beneath an active volcano, a young nanny ("Dreamchild's" Nicola Cowper) and two teenage brothers are caught in cave-in that plunges them all the way down into the lost city of Atlantis! Featuring a dazzling array of special effects and exotic locales, this fantasy-thriller is a dizzying trip into outlandish adventure and cliff-hanger excitement!

BEHOLD! Not since the beautiful oeuvre of ROBO VAMPIRE's mastermind Godfrey Ho has a film been so Frankenstein-ed into a snarling horror of incomprehensibility!

The story goes that screenwriter Rusty Lemorande (what a name!) started directing a family-friendly adaption of Jules Verne's JOURNEY TO THE CENTRE OF THE EARTH in the style of Jim Henson's LABYRINTH. The poster for Rusty's version promised puppets, adventure and Emo Phillips. Unfortunately, for reasons I couldn't discern in my research (Money? Time? Skill?), the production was shut down, but Cannon had already cashed the cheques from the pre-sales, so a product had to be delivered. CUT TO: Albert Pyun takes on the arduous task of finishing the film, I assume, because he suggested that he could use the underground sets still standing from his previous Cannon production ALIEN FROM L.A. But his recycling didn't stop there. Instead of continuing the story of the original JOURNEY shoot, he decided to concoct a side-sequel to ALIEN FROM L.A. and brought in Simon Poland, Janie du Plessis and Lochner de Kock to reprise their roles of Hairdresser, Rykov/Shank and Professor Ovid Galba from ALIEN. Yes, it's as confusing as it sounds.

JOURNEY's plot seems straightforward at first: A twenty-something British nanny (Nicola Cowper), a dog, and a lunkhead man (Paul Carafotes) with his younger siblings (Jaclyn Bernstein and Ilan Mitchell-Smith) go exploring a cave in Hawaii when a volcano

explodes and traps them underground. The first act of the film seems to be from the original shoot, and it's surprisingly miserable as the gang trudge through the caverns dying of thirst, complaining, and hoping to be saved. One by one they are removed from the story (never to be seen again) until only the nanny and the younger brother are left, probably because they were the only cast members that agreed to come back for the re-shoots. Suddenly, both of them fall through a hole and find themselves separated on the Atlantis sets from ALIEN FROM L.A. They never meet up again.

"WHAT THE HELL WAS THAT?"
- EVERYONE WHO HAS EVER WATCHED JOURNEY TO THE CENTRE OF THE EARTH

It's unclear what footage is left over from the original shoot. Pyun has said in interviews that he only had ten usable minutes to work with, but one could assume that everything before the Atlantis section (about 45 minutes) was from the previous version of the film. To be honest, I could also be wrong as the earlier part does have a very Pyun-like quality to it, and it is set in his home state of Hawaii. There's only one scene that is definitely from the first shoot, and I know that because, at one point, a character drifts off to sleep and the audience witnesses a dream that features a dozen big articulated creatures, a massive set, and radically different costumes. And Emo Phillips is there too! The scene is shot in a loose, less confident style, that seems uncomfortable with the effects work. The sleeping character wakes up, the dream ends, and the viewer never sees anything like that again. Instead, the back half of the film is a baffling collection of moments that assumes the audience is very familiar with ALIEN FROM L.A. To add insult to injury, nothing gets resolved. A confusing climax plays out, there's a freeze frame in the middle of a scene, and it's followed by a harsh cut to a character watching TV in his home (with no reference how he got there) to wrap things with seventy minutes on the clock. Cue a music video and fifteen minutes of credit. Shameless.

I don't doubt that Albert Pyun stepped into the project on his own accord. Pyun has filled his career with daredevil schemes where he tried to pull off the impossible, whether it was shooting a film in three days (DECEIT) or trying to make two mega productions back to back on the same set (the never-shot SPIDER-MAN and MASTERS OF THE UNIVERSE 2). I'm awed by his confidence, but can't in good faith praise the result. I don't know if the shambling patchwork job was due to money issues, miscommunication or creative clashes, but it's pretty embarrassing. At least hackmeister extraordinaire Godfrey Ho (of NINJA TERMINATOR fame) had the decency of having two unrelated pictures run parallel to each other and deliver a climax! Here, the reappearance of a few actors only makes the rest of the movie extra puzzling. Pyun removed his name from the finished version of JOURNEY and disowned the project, which only makes me wonder if he had a more elaborate plan when the plug got pulled? What could it have possibly been? I would only recommend watching the film if you're curious to see what Cannon was brazen enough to release with a straight face.

CYBORG (1989)

CAST
Jean-Claude Van Damme, Deborah Richter, Vincent Klyn

WRITER
Albert Pyun (as Kitty Chalmers)

PRODUCERS
Yoram Globus, Menahem Golan

CINEMATOGRAPHER
Philip Alan Waters

EDITORS
Scott Stevenson, Rozanne Zingale, Sheldon Lettich (Uncredited), Jean-Claude Van Damme (Uncredited)

MUSIC
Kevin Bassinson

COSTUME DESIGN
Heidi Kaczenski

PRODUCTION DESIGNER
Douglas H. Leonard

RUNTIME
86 mins

BACK OF THE BOX "BLOODSPORT" martial arts wizard JEAN-CLAUDE VAN DAMME carves out a dazzling new domain as the future's most fearsome warrior in this sweeping sword and sci-fi adventure epic. Convulsed by social anarchy and a virulent, incurable plague, twenty-first century America has descended into a seething, barbaric nightmare. On a desperate quest for data to cure the epidemic, a beautiful human-robot Cyborg is captured by cannibalistic Flesh Pirates, out to keep the cure for themselves. Now, only the awesome fighting skills of the sword-for-hire Gibson Rickenbacker (JEAN-CLAUDE VAN DAMME) can rescue her - and save what remains of civilization. From the director of "THE SWORD AND THE SORCERER", "CYBORG" delivers an explosive, future shocked bloody battle against the ultimate evil.

EVERYONE reading this knows Jean-Claude Van Damme's CYBORG. It has come to define the era of silly sci-fi action films on which Cannon made their stock in trade. It's got the nonsensical goofy title, a lead who can barely speak any English, and some clunky, heavy-handed direction. We've all universally accepted there's a concise way to describe a movie in that mould: Dumb.

No one wants to be called dumb. Even when used as a term of endearment, it comes with negative connotations. It's a word that we use to raise ourselves above something that we enjoyed. We want to prove that we're smarter than the people that made it. It's a coward's gambit, and I say this with the full awareness that I use it all the time.

"IT WAS SO MUCH FUN, BUT MAN, IT WAS SO DUMB!"

Dumb, in my eyes, is a decision made without thought. It could be a choice that betrays your perception of what's "logical" in entertainment and torpedoes any chance of enjoyment. That's fine. Movies are individual experiences, and we all absorb them differently.

BUT IF YOU ENJOY CYBORG, PLEASE DON'T CALL IT DUMB.

You can call it silly, crazy, wacky, goofy or any other modifiers you can think up. You can even call it lazy! Just not dumb.

Here's a list of things that people have called dumb over the years:

- Video Games
- Comic Books
- Horror
- Action
- Adventure
- Science-Fiction
- Fantasy

All because those things didn't fit the image of what "real" entertainment is supposed to be. Or "real" art. Or "real" whatever. If it's silly or over the top, it can't just be good, right? Even if you love it whole-heartedly, you gotta throw in that dumb modifier or people may think you're dumb as well!

I don't even feel particularly strongly about the release version CYBORG.

You can feel the producers trying to make it something it's not. They desperately want to fool the viewer into believing it's a rousing adventure story instead of the downbeat Japanese ronin film Pyun had shot. The "fixes" sand away all the hard edges, smooth out the narrative and the final score by Kevin Bassinson, which is all MIDI bells and drum beats, underlines the dumbness of the whole project.

And even with all that meddling, Van Damme is still at his physical prime. I'm impressed by the film's patience (which frustrated me to no end on my first viewing) The colour cinematography by Philip Alan Waters pops with stark oranges and blues that give the Post-Apocalyptic night an impressive mood.

I know a lot of people would disagree with me. You're allowed to have an opinion, but do you mind me asking...

WHY DO YOU THINK CYBORGS ARE DUMB?

WHY IS SOMEONE DOING THE SPLITS TO GET THE DROP ON A BAD GUY DUMB?

WHY IS A BIG BURLY DUDE IN WRAP-AROUND SHADES DUMB?

If you hate it, then it's dumb. If you like it and get enjoyment out of it, why not try to use another word? You can even find some decisions in the film dumb, but to slap the entire feature with that label is unfair. I don't mean to come off as holier than thou. I call things dumb all the time! And sometimes I mean it nicely! It's easy, but it also paints things in an unfair light that has more repercussions than you'd think.

DECEIT (1990)

CAST
Samantha Phillips, Norbert Weisser, Scott Paulin

WRITER
Albert Pyun (As Kitty Chalmers)

PRODUCER
Tom Karnowski

CINEMATOGRAPHER
Philip Alan Waters

MUSIC
Anthony Riparetti, James Saad

PRODUCTION DESIGNER
Douglas H. Leonard

EDITOR
Sydney Conrad Shapiro

COSTUME DESIGN
(Uncredited)

RUNTIME
90 mins

BACK OF THE BOX Offbeat and wildly original, DECEIT stars Scott Paulin and Norbert Weisser as Bailey and Brick, two sex fiend "aliens" dispatched to destroy the Earth. Trained by their planet's Environmental Protection Agency to destroy polluter planets, Bailey and Brick specialize in seducing the native women of each planet they vaporize. But the newest object of their affection, a prostitute named Eve (Samantha Phillips) rebuffs their advances, sending them into intergalactic fits of fury. A raucous, razor edged satire that pokes fun at sex, science fiction, and the ozone, DECEIT bravely goes where no movie has gone before.

I'M ALWAYS AMAZED by the directors who can make a film with no money or time and somehow still pull it off like a well-choreographed heist. Fred Olen Ray's HOLLYWOOD CHAINSAW HOOKERS (1988) may not be a great film, but I love the fact that Ray was able to finish it over a weekend, with a lot of favours and a ton of courage.

The story goes that Pyun was unhappy with his experience on CYBORG. He had made a pessimistic black and white acid western called SLINGER, but Jean-Claude Van Damme and the producers wanted a tonally similar follow-up to Cannon's surprise hit BLOODSPORT. After many arguments, Pyun was strong-armed into doing re-shoots for CYBORG, and in retaliation, he cooked up an impossible plan: He would make an entirely new feature film with the resources for the pick-ups. Pyun wrote an original script called DECEIT, picked a location for the re-shoots that would meet DECEIT's needs, and got the production to rent the gear for a week. He wrapped CYBORG's shoot on a Thursday night, and because the camera rental house didn't expect the equipment to be returned until Monday, Pyun had three full days to do whatever he wanted as long as his actors never did more than one take and he kept the budget under $22,000.

You can't shoot much in three days that isn't pornography or a filmed stage play, so Pyun settled on a variation of the latter. His idea (writing under the pseudonym Kitty Chalmers) was about a bunch of weirdos that picks up a hitchhiker (Norbert Weisser) who then murders everyone except a woman (Samantha Phillips). The hitchhiker traps her in a warehouse and admits that he's an alien who is going to destroy the planet in an hour. Also, he really wants to have sex with her.

The alien angle sounds goofy, but it doesn't mask a grim set-up that could have quickly turned down a torture porn-ish road, especially when the woman is forced to undress at gunpoint. Thankfully, the woman turns the tables on her captor. She refuses to pleasure him physically, and when he "reads her mind" and accuses her of being a slut, she reacts furiously and points out that he has no idea who she is, despite his psychic powers. Before the viewer's eyes, the victim becomes the alpha as she verbally pummels her intergalactic captor until he's revealed to be nothing more than a pitiful "nice guy" who desperately wants to get laid as a form of validation. Pyun pushes things a little bit too far in terms of threatening abuse, but just when things look like they're about to take a gross turn, the story pivots. The hitchhiker admits he has a mental health problem and everything he said was a lie. And then another man shows up (Scott Paulin) who claims to be a doctor. Have they all escaped from a mental asylum? Did the radio really say that a nuclear war had started?

While the script half-heartedly tries to play up some ambiguity, it's pretty apparent early on that Pyun is going full sci-fi. Yes, the two men are aliens, and yes, the earth is about to be destroyed for a reason consistent with Pyun's world view. The film is less about what's

true, but who will convince who? Will the two men, both of them representing different extremes, be able to gaslight the woman into believing their lies?

The emphasis on circular David Mamet-ish dialogue may aggravate some viewers, but it kept me engrossed. Veteran Pyun performers Norbert Weisser and Scott Paulin do an admirable job as the two aliens (one crazy, the other slick) and Samantha Phillips pulls her weight as the emotional center, whose thrown from belief to doubt over and over again, without ever losing a sense of self. Pyun limits his shot selection to a few set-ups, but they're always visually appealing, and the primary location sports a giant oscillating fan that beautifully illuminates some picturesque shafts of dusty light.

Pyun could have easily phoned in a product that played up the exploitative elements. Instead, he took a big swing at delivering a movie with a strong feminist message (a reoccurring theme in his work) that highlights the strength and independence of his female lead. The skeezy men may try to take advantage of her — by force and bribery — but they're undone because she's stronger and more empathetic than both of them combined. It's a noble goal, rendered a little problematic when the film demands the protagonist be stripped to her bra and panties for most of its running time. Still, I'm glad Pyun attempted it, and the film's final moments are impressive as a direct FUCK YOU to a misogynist world.

I'd be willing to bet money that Pyun drew inspiration from Edgar G. Ulmer's poverty row classic DETOUR (1945) to make his similarly-titled production. Both share an impoverished production history (Ulmer claimed he shot DETOUR in six days for $20,000), and the parallel story elements (the hitchhiker, a man and a woman in a battle of wits) seem too similar to be a coincidence. Just like Ulmer's film, DECEIT is an articulation of its director's tortured state of mind — like his protagonist, Pyun felt trapped and under siege by smooth talkers that wanted to convince him his instincts were wrong.

DECEIT is one of the rare gambles Pyun was able to pull off successfully. He shot 13,000 feet of film, edited the picture (which came out to 10,000 feet), and sold it to Menahem Golan. Sadly, it didn't make much of a splash and is rarely discussed. I hope its fascinating back-story provides enough mystique to motivate the curious to check it out.

FUN FACT The people on the video box are nowhere to be seen in the film.

CAPTAIN AMERICA (1990)

CAST
Matt Salinger, Ronny Cox, Ned Beatty

WRITER
Stephen Tolkin

PRODUCER
Menahem Golan

CINEMATOGRAPHER
Philip Alan Waters

MUSIC
Barry Goldberg

PRODUCTION DESIGNER
Douglas H. Leonard

EDITOR
Jon Poll

COSTUME DESIGN
Heidi Kaczenski

RUNTIME
97 mins

BACK OF THE BOX California, 1930, Steve Rogers (Matt Salinger) is selected for the top secret "Operation Rebirth" programme. Injected with a serum that dramatically increases his strength and issued with an imposing form-fitting uniform, Steve is transformed from an All-American homeboy into an All-American Hero. Pitched against Hitler's own human weapon, Red Skull, Captain America is overpowered and sent crashing on a missile in the frozen Arctic wastes. Now, 40 years later, the perfectly preserved Captain America is revived from his icy bed and returns to his fight with the Red Skull, who is still the maniac master mastermind behind most of the world's evil. In the best tradition of super heroes, Captain America leaps out of the comic pages and onto the screen in this all action adventure story of good versus evil.

ALBERT PYUN DARES TO ANSWER A QUESTION NO ONE ASKED:
WHAT IF CAPTAIN AMERICA WAS A LOSER?

"Can you pull the car over? I'm going to be sick." - Our hero before he steals a vehicle from 53-year Ned Beatty.

MATT SALINGER (the son of reclusive author J.D.) stars as an ancient-looking teenage soldier who is injected with superhero serum, wears a goofy rubber suit and fails at his first mission. He takes a deep freeze nap in the arctic and wakes up in the 1990s lost and confused. Cap's nemesis (who he only faces once before he's frozen), the Italian Red Skull (Scott Paulin), kidnaps the President of the United States (Ronny Cox) for daring to propose a Green New Deal (really!). So, Captain America stumbles into an accidental rescue mission. If you haven't caught on yet, this Cap is not the steadfast and experienced hero of the comics. Sure, he can still punch a dude, flip through the air and throw a hilariously plastic shield, but Pyun's version of the

character has zero experience and continuously has his bacon saved by the supporting cast. Cap's main superpower is pretending to be sick while in a car, and when the driver gets out to see if he's okay, Captain America: The First Avenger jumps behind the wheel and zooms off. This ruse happens twice! TWICE! A desperate person with something to prove could analyze the production as a wry satirical commentary on the ineptitude of America on the world stage — that for all its conceptual hero making myths, it's really a joke to everyone who stares at it dead on.

Or a viewer could also throw up their hands and scream, "This movie sucks!"

THE AUTHOR IS DEAD AND ALL THAT.

It's undeniable that the film fails as a Captain America adaptation. Matt Salinger has the generic look of a square-jawed hero, but he's also got a puffy goofball vibe which is augmented tenfold when he dons the blue gimp suit to give a shaky thumbs-up. The script does him no favours either, with a start and stop pace that includes a gaggle of unfocused subplots wrestling for screen time: There's the daughter of Cap's old flame, the presence of Ned Beatty as a can-do reporter, and even the Red Skull has a troublesome offspring. It all comes together in a narrative that swerves from unearned Norman Rockwell sentimentality to a winded Captain America being chased by generic 80s goons on dirt bikes.

It feels rushed and stretched out at the same time, with Cap never getting a chance to be a proactive hero and forever being caught unprepared as his loved ones are killed around him. Pyun does manage to deliver a few fun Cap action scenes in a wide-angle comic book style where Matt Salinger's Italian double flips and punches his way through stuntmen. Scott Paulin, as the Red Skull, does get to bring some operatic ham to his portrayal. He sports a surprisingly effective Red Skull make-up job that's accentuated by dead grey eyes, but then for some mystifying reason, after the prologue, he spends the rest of the film in flesh-coloured make-up that makes him look like a third tier Dick Tracy villain.

Cannon's production of CAPTAIN AMERICA is infamous for being a massive boondoggle. At one point it was going to be directed by Michael Winner (DEATH WISH) based on a baffling script where Cap was an artist, and the Red Skull wanted to steal the statue of liberty, but when Winner dropped the project, team player/punching-bag Pyun took the reins. Marvel wouldn't let Pyun cast two actors to portray the pre- and post-superhero serum caps (Pyun wanted Football star Howie Long as the muscular Cap). Par for the course, Pyun was promised a reasonable budget, and right before the shooting began, Cannon slashed it and forced him to rush through filming in Yugoslavia. The producers told Pyun he could flesh out the action scenes when they got to LA, but they lied (again!) and took the picture out of his hands. Cannon delivered a barely coherent cut and released it to gales of public laughter. Pyun swears to this day he's never seen the final release version.

Even with all my complaints, I feel like there's still value to be found in this bastard child. The 90s Cap has got a fun globe-trotting vibe, the campiness works if you're in the right mood, and the bursts of action are truly enjoyable. Whether you like superhero films or not, it's undeniable that Marvel Studios has settled into a formula, so it's refreshing to watch a bumbling goof try to take down the Red Skull. Ronny Cox as a president who idolizes Cap is a smart idea, the plastic shield has a deadly weight, and while I don't think the Red Skull's new Italian back-story works, it's an interesting way to approach the character. In a world where there was no Captain America film, Cannon's version felt like an insult to the fans. In a pop culture landscape that features six loyal portrayals of the character on the big screen, there's no harm hanging out with the loser version for 90 minutes. Somebody's gotta do it.

FUN FACT For a hot second, Pyun was also attached to Cannon's ill-fated production of SPIDER-MAN. The film had the web-slinger squaring off against a random vampire (no, not Morbius from the comics), and Pyun wanted to shoot HE-MAN 2 and SPIDER-MAN simultaneously on the same sets. The projects flopped before shooting began, but some sets had been built, so Pyun used them to make CYBORG

INTERVIEW
NORBERT WEISSER
(ACTOR)

If you don't mind starting from the beginning, how did you first get into acting?

I started out in the theatre way back in 1969 with a group that demonstrated against the war in Vietnam, after that, I worked in the Odyssey Theater and toured all around Europe. We were young and had a lot of ideas, so I started knocking on doors at the Hollywood studios. In those days you could just walk in and leave pictures, so I started doing some television work as a guest and co-star. My first movie was MIDNIGHT EXPRESS, and that put me on that map in 1977.

Did you make a conscious decision to be a film and television actor?

I never really left the theatre. Let's put it this way, in TV and movies the money is extraordinary. I hardly ever said no. In theatre, I only did what I wanted to do. I even approached some theatres with "How about we do this?"

Do you remember the first time you met Albert Pyun?

It was on RADIOACTIVE DREAMS (1985). I did the audition at a studio, and we just sat and talked. He liked me, and we hit it off from there.

What was your experience like on RADIOACTIVE DREAMS?

I only worked a few days on it, but I felt like I nailed the character, and he loved it. I found out afterwards about all the problems they ran into, essentially money problems, but I wasn't there to witness it. I just did my stuff, so I had a blast. There was no stress I could feel. He was just digging on me and letting me do whatever I want to do, so I went to town. The only thing that bothered me, was that the sound in my scene had to be completely dubbed, and you never get the moment that was happening when you dub. It doesn't come from your inner self, it becomes a technical thing.

Did you get a sense you'd work with Albert again?

Not really. We liked each other. We knew we'd like to work with each other again, and from there, I never read for him again. Ever. He would just call me and go, "How about this character?" He cast me as all kinds of different characters. Most directors figure who you are and cast you based on who they believe you can play. Albert gave me everything. The wimpy character. The hero. Insane people. It was a joy to work with him. I think the next one was DOWN TWISTED (1987)?

Yep!

That was shot in Mexico. and everyone got along. The only problem was that some disease hit our hotel, and we all had to deliver some fecal matter for testing. But it was a good shoot. After that on CAPTAIN AMERICA (1990), it was just a phone call, and I shot for one quick day.

How did DECEIT (1990) come about?

Albert just needs to go, go, go. He gets bored. He dropped off the script for DECEIT and said, "I have short ends from CYBORG, I have a set I can use from the movie, I've got the crew, so all I need you to do is get some people to be in it, and we'll shoot it on the weekend" I cast Scott Paulin, and Albert cast Samantha Phillips. She was a delight. She came to my house, and we rehearsed together.

Was there a feeling that it was a secret shoot? I read that the CYBORG production didn't know it was going on.

Well, he was using some of the crew from CYBORG, and he didn't want the producers to know. There was often only one take on DECEIT. We came in fully rehearsed and shot through the night.

Was it a stressful shoot with that kind of time crunch?

There were times where if you didn't hit your mark, you were screwed. There's one monologue where I'm almost in the dark because I didn't land in the right spot! But it didn't matter! We just went on. After he cut the film, it wasn't long enough, so he wrote an opening scene where I take poison and kill myself. It was just wild. Whatever works! We shot that part outside with no permits. The cops came around the second we finished, and we went "Uh, we were just leaving," and got away! And Albert sold DECEIT in Cannes *(to Cannon Films).*

Do you remember much about ARCADE (1991)?

What I remember is that I had a bit of attitude on that shoot. I was working a lot, and I had a chip on my shoulder about sharing a dressing room. Not just because I'm an asshole, which I've been known to sometimes be, but I kind of thought "Come on. I need privacy when I work." I don't like to share my space with strangers. It doesn't feel good. But you know, it wasn't bad! I remember there was a long monologue and I had to do several takes. In retrospect, I liked what I did.

How you describe Albert's directing style?

It would mostly be technical. Where he wants you. He didn't screw around. He never told me what to do or how he wanted it played, at least I certainly don't remember that from him. He does have a thing that can be slightly annoying, which that he's moving the second CUT is yelled. There's no 'That was great' because he's already gone.

Were there any films Albert offered you that you turned down?

There were several movies I wish I had done because I liked them. I was supposed to play a part in POSTMORTEM, but they said I'd have to fly myself up there, and I just went "Fuck that." In retrospect, I should have gone because I'm usually interested as long as it pays for itself and I don't have to pay into it. There's one I said, "No" to, and he pushed me into it anyway. I was doing THE ROAD TO WELLVILLE (1994) with Alan Parker, and Albert changed the script of his next film on me with only two days before I had to get on a plane and go shoot with him in the Philippines. It was a kickboxing film...

HEATSEEKER (1995)?

Right! That's it! I said I can't do it. I need time to learn lines. And he just said, "Look, the first few days, you just do the old script, we work around it, and as you do the old one you can learn the new lines." I said okay because I always felt safe with him. He was on my side. He never wanted me to feel like a jerk. I got through it! Sometimes I'd have lines taped to the desk.

It must have been a lot to remember. You're the main villain in that film.

That was a wonderful shoot. Everyone got along, I think he was happy, and he was doing three movies in six weeks all over the world.

He must have moved really fast on things like NEMESIS 3: TIME-LAPSE (1996).

On that one, we were in a huge mineshaft place, and we'd drive around in go-carts. For some reason, there was a whole section where I was naked. Albert would push me sometimes and ask, "Will you do that?" and I would go, "I don't give a shit! Make me naked!" You don't even see it in the movie! At one point they left me completely alone, I got dressed, and I was a half-mile away from everyone else.

ADRENALIN: FEAR THE RUSH (1996) was produced by Miramax and was going to be released in theatres. Was there a sense that it was going to be a bigger movie than usual?

I really liked the original script. There was a sparseness to it, but they wanted it to look like a higher budget movie, and they forced Albert into re-writes that he didn't want to do. I think the movie lost something because of it, but I have great memories of the shoot. We shot in a dungeon. It was below the most beautiful castle that had a museum in it. I recall a magical morning where he shot us coming into a building, but outside there was a forest and horses walking around and eating grass. The early light came in, and it was magical. I do know Albert had trouble from the money people. It's supposed to be a story about people under severe threat, but the final version doesn't have any of that. I was one of the few people that had a rough cut on tape and Albert used it for the release he put out himself.

NEMESIS 4 (1996) was also shot in a few days during the re-shoots for ADRENALIN: FEAR THE RUSH. Did you have any problems with shooting two films at once?

Well, I'm not particularly fast on learning lines. My friends are getting older and are going through that now, and I'm like 'Welcome to the club! I've lived there." I got the script for NEMESIS 4 when I got off the plane for the ADRENALIN re-shoots, and I remember there's one long monologue right before the star of the film (Susan Price) kills me with her tits. I needed someone to do lines with, so when I was free, Albert got some local students to help me out. Even if I struggled sometimes, I felt completely safe with Albert. I couldn't go wrong with him. If I blew a take, which I hate, it was fine. It didn't rattle him.

He sounds like a director that never lost his cool on set.

Never.

Any memories from BLAST (1997)?

The shoot was fun. It was probably a week long, and it was nice to do something in America. All the stuff I did outside of America doesn't get me residuals.

Really?

I don't even get residuals from SCHINDLER'S LIST!

That's crazy!

Yeah! I spent three months on that movie. They hired me out of Munich. They pay you per shooting day. The first offer Spielberg's people gave me was so low that it would have cost me to go and be in the film. I would be in the red. I had to say no to a Spielberg movie! Eventually, they figured it out.

Do you ever get recognized from any of your roles?

Not really. I often get people looking at me and going, "I know you from somewhere," but that's about it. I remember being in my car in the '70s going down the freeway at 85mph and looking over and seeing people in the next car screaming "MIDDDDDNNNNIGHHHHT EXPPPPPRESSS" at me.

Have you kept in touch with any of the other Pyun Players?

Me and Thom Mathews still keep in touch. Some of them I cast myself, like Scott Paulin, and we're close friends. What usually happens is that you have a certain amount of friends in life and that's it, and while you have intense experiences on set, you go on and do your own thing.

How was your experience on CRAZY SIX (1997)?

I got along very well with Burt Reynolds! Whoever you think he is, that's who he is. He's kind of guy's guy. The way he delivers his lines is how he acts. Just a nice guy. He was a stunt man, so he can take shit.

How were your interactions with the stars on Albert's pictures?

I got along with all the stars. You shoot a movie together, and everyone's just a bunch of people. These guys knew they were on a downward trend. They used to be big movie stars, and they knew the business could be humbling. I can tell you something about my time on OMEGA DOOM (1996): Rutger Hauer is a tricky guy. He doesn't act like a star, but he does listen to a different drummer. Rutger would start drinking at around seven. I was playing a decapitated head in that movie, just sitting there talking to him, and around seven he'd go "That's it. I'm out of here," and leave. They'd turn round on me, and I'd do the entire scene with a script girl, but I didn't hold it against him. There are some times where I need other actors. That was not one of those times. If it were dramatic, I'd demand it. Albert always made sure I had the other actor if I needed them. Me and Rutger got along, but as I said, he was tricky. I did another movie with him, and he did the same thing (AMELIA EARHART: THE FINAL FLIGHT) I had my close up, and Rutger went "We don't need a close-up for that. Let's do it as a two-shot," and I said "No, let's do my close-up" and the director backed me up.

After that, there was an all-green screen movie called SORCERERS (1998).

I wish that came out. It was based on THE THREE MUSKETEERS, and he shot it out of pocket. I loved the character I played. He had one eye that was blind. He was just the most nebbish little scaredy little motherfucker that you can imagine, like nothing I have ever played. I loved my performance in that one, but he was going to do the special effects himself, and never got the money for it, so it never went anywhere. He went back a few years ago to see if he could still solve the problems, but I think he gave up again. It was one of the roles I went "Yeah! I nailed it"

What was the mood on the TICKER (2001)? I heard it was a very strained shoot for Albert.

That was a tricky one. He was being mistreated by Steven Seagal, who's a real difficult guy, and Tom Sizemore, who I think is a fabulous actor, but was on his way down with a drinking problem. They kind of teamed up together against him, and Albert had a hard time controlling them. He sweat and suffered on that shoot. It was very difficult.

Do you recall working on BAD BIZNESS (2003)?

He saved my life on that picture. My son Morgan had a really serious drug addiction, and I was falling apart, and Albert was doing that film in Hawaii, and he said "Come, you need a break, all you can do now is worry, so come take a break," so I did. Albert was so kind,

he knew what I was going through, and he helped me get through that nightmare. And after that, I got together with my son, and he went into detox. My son is seventeen years clean sober now.

I'm so glad to hear that. Your son Morgan appears in INVASION (2005) with you.

Albert gave me that script, and he said he wanted to do it in one shot, so I brought in Scott Paulin, his wife, his daughter and my son. And I got a producer credit! It was shot in one day. We had only one night. First of all, the rain wouldn't stop, and the place where we were shooting was flooded, so we were holding on for two weeks without filming. Finally, Albert said, let's do it. We only had that night left, and in the middle of the first take, someone blew it. There was enough darkness for one more take. It was a nightmare of moving actors around from spot to spot. I remember the car I was in drove me to the very end and it died, but it died at the right time! We got it somehow. We would not have been able to do it again! The money people at Lionsgate, said: "Why did this cop have an accent?" and my friend had to re-dub my performance. This was a problem I often ran into. That's why I liked Albert. He didn't care I had an accent! He'd say, "Just go with it."

COOL AIR (2006) also feels like a family affair. Morgan stars in it.

That's another one we did by the seat of our pants in a few days at the producer's house. Again, I got to play a character I had never played before and never played since, and you know, I feel warm to it, but I feel warm toward all of Albert's movies. I'm not very critical in the way I usually am. They're Albert Pyun films!

Did you ever get a sense that Albert was going to stop making movies?

He can't. He will die making a movie. He started out when he was a kid. He would lasso all his buddies and make films with their Super 8 camera, and that's where he is now. He's gone full circle. Now, with much more sophisticated equipment and more knowledge, but he will make movies until he can't walk. That's a story I think is beautiful. There's something about that's very impressive, unusual and moving in Hollywood.

THE GOLDEN PERIOD

KICKBOXER 2 (1991) - NEMESIS 2 (1995)

Pyun was at full strength during The Golden Period. He had money to work with, he collaborated with an extremely skilled crew, and his imagination was firing on all cylinders. The period includes one of his most accomplished films (NEMESIS), the two pictures he made for Full Moon Features (DOLLMAN and ARCADE) and the three movies he shot in quick succession around the world (SPITFIRE, HEATSEEKER, and HONG KONG '97).

KICK BOXER 2: THE ROAD BACK (1991)

CAST
Sasha Mitchell, Peter Boyle, Dennis Chan

WRITER
David S. Goyer

PRODUCER
Tom Karnowski

CINEMATOGRAPHER
George Mooradian

MUSIC
Anthony Riparetti, James Saad

PRODUCTION DESIGNER
Nicholas T. Preovolos

EDITOR
Alan Baumgarten

COSTUME DESIGN
Joseph A. Porro

RUNTIME
89 mins

BACK OF THE BOX Humiliated by his defeat at the hands of Kurt Sloan, deadly Thai warrior Tong Po returns for revenge and kills his powerful adversary. But, realizing that he has also destroyed any chance of regaining his honour in a rematch, the only hope now lies in luring Kurt's brother, and former kickboxing champion, David back into the arena. And when the opponents finally come face to face, fist bound and dipped in broken glass, the ultimate confrontation will be decided in a bloody battle that can have only one survivor! PUT UP, SHUT UP... OR DIE!

I DON'T KNOW HOW Albert Pyun found the strength to keep making movies. I have trouble getting out of bed on the best of days, and Pyun somehow rose at the crack of dawn for thirty years to tackle impossible projects that were destined to be derided by the public. Perhaps he was an eternal optimist who had the phrase, "The next one will be better" forever at the forefront of his mind. It's the only way I can imagine someone could handle being called the "World's worst director" and "This Generation's Ed Wood" with depressing regularity. How did he not fall into a crushing depression and take a desk job? The money can't have been that good!

WELL, I NEVER EXPECTED TO FIND THE ANSWER IN A KICKBOXER SEQUEL, BUT HERE WE ARE.

KICKBOXER 2: THE ROAD BACK is about the third Sloan brother, David (Sasha Mitchell), who runs a gym for underprivileged youth in LA. JCVD (the star of the first KICKBOXER) died off-screen between films and David just wants to get on with his life. Everyone knows he's a great fighter, but he still can't make rent, so in a last-ditch effort to keep the gym open, he takes a match from a shady promoter (Peter Boyle). David quickly wins the match, but promptly announces his retirement, and in retaliation, a mysterious Thai sponsor (Cary-Hiroyuki Tagawa) burns David's gym to the ground.

Crippled and demoralized, David decides to spend the rest of his life in bed.

The original Jean-Claude Van Damme KICKBOXER (1989) upped the ante on the goofiest parts of BLOODSPORT, and I had hoped the follow-up would do the same. Instead, KICKBOXER 2 proved to be a sombre meditation on falling and struggling to get back up. And it only had three fights! When I watched it years ago, I wrote it off as a bore.

On this viewing, I quickly realized the reason I had found it so dull the first time around: I expected an action film and Pyun had made a drama. The story isn't about David learning a secret move to defeat the bad guy (which he does, of course), or proving that he is the strongest. It's more interested in David mustering up the mental strength to do something as simple as leaving his apartment. The big training montage isn't about building up the power for the showdown. It's literally about learning to walk again. There are no easy words of wisdom that will save the day. The only thing that can keep him going is the support of those around him. That's super refreshing to find in a sub-genre that's mostly made up of "JUST FIGHT HARDER!" mantras.

While Van Damme was all muscle, Sasha Mitchell's David moves like a snake — always shifting his shoulders from side to side — as he speaks in a down-to-earth tone of voice. You genuinely feel like he wants to do the right thing as the world crushes him at every turn. KICKBOXER 2 is one of Pyun's slicker affairs, without much visual experimentation, but it still sports a beautiful magic-hour look thanks to cinematographer George Mooradian in his first feature collaboration with Albert. There's a real lived-in feel to the film's depiction of the rougher sections of LA, but it never comes off like caricature. Sure, strip clubs are abundant, but there's also a park nearby where the community practices Tai-Chi.

The picture's most significant stylistic conceit is that the fights are executed entirely in slow motion, which makes them feel more like Passion Plays than martial arts combat. The good guys exist only to be brutally pummelled RAGING BULL-style. Their strength lies not merely in being heroic but in somehow finding the will to keep going when everything seems hopeless — without ever feeling the need to keep pushing out of mere pride or honour — because moving forward for egotistical reasons is toxic. It's a surprisingly mature concept for a franchise whose most famous moment is JCVD doing a sexy dance.

I may be making KICKBOXER 2 sound like made-for-TV production ("Tonight: The Martial Artist That Fought For His Heart on ABC"), but it's also a surprisingly faithful sequel in terms of continuing the storyline and bringing back characters, like Dennis Chan's master and Tong Po, the villain from the first film.

And while THE ROAD BACK reads like a non sequitur subtitle at first, the film is actually interested in portraying an arduous journey that can only be a traversed with time, mental/physical rehabilitation, and the support of others. How does someone find the will to keep going? Not just the desire to win, but the intangible strength one must continually nurture to be able to thrive.

How did Albert Pyun do it?

FUN FACT The script was written by young David Goyer who would later go on to write the BLADE trilogy and MAN OF STEEL. His early credits also include the Charlie Band productions DEMONIC TOYS and ARCADE (which Pyun directed).

SAD FACT Pyun never gave up. For example, on CAPTAIN AMERICA, the money was so tight that on some days there would be no film for the camera. Pyun said he'd still shoot scenes and pretend nothing was wrong because he knew if he shut down the production, it would never start up again. Now that's perseverance.

BLOODMATCH (1991)

CAST
Thom Mathews, Hope Marie Carlton, Marianne Taylor

WRITER
K. Hannah (Probable pseudonym of Albert Pyun)

PRODUCERS
Rick Blumenthal, Corinne Olivo

CINEMATOGRAPHER
George Mooradian

MUSIC
Paul Edwards, Anthony Riparetti

PRODUCTION DESIGNER
(uncredited)

EDITOR
Paul O'Bryan

COSTUME DESIGN
Cindy Rosenthal

RUNTIME
86 mins

BACK OF THE BOX Bloodmatch presents the most awesome group of world champion kickboxers ever to be seen on screen including Benny "The Jet" Urquidez in a story of one man's deadly search for revenge. Brick Bardo (Thom Mathews) wants to know who killed his brother - and he'll go to any lengths to find out the truth. Five years earlier, one of the four kickboxing champions was fixing fights and set up his brother in the fight that took his life. Could it be Mike Johnson (Thunder Wolf) Brent Caldwell (Dale Jacoby); Billy Munoz (Benny "The Jet" Urquidez) or Connie Angel (Hope Marie Carlton)? There's only one way for Bardo to find out - he meets them in the ring for an all-out fight to the finish that will call on all their skills to survive. Punching, kicking, gouging, there are no-holds-barred as one man takes on four of the meanest, toughest kickboxers alive in his search for justice. Who killed Brick Bardo's brother? The answer will surprise you - the battle will devastate you.

"DEATH IS A GAME NOBODY PLAYS TWICE"

Soak up that funny tag line. It's the only fun you'll be having with this one.

In the first scene of BLOODMATCH, Brick Bardo (Thom Mathews) tortures a man in the desert for nine agonizing minutes. And when I say agonizing, I'm not drawing comparisons to the unflinching style of someone like Writer/Director Michael Haneke (FUNNY GAMES). No, I mean that it goes on endlessly for no discernible reason. "Why is he still talking?" will cross your mind, and, "What else are we going to learn here?" The answer is simple: A distributor won't accept a film unless it's around 90 minutes.

From the desert, we're slowly, ever so slowly, introduced to all five main characters in vignettes that waffle between protracted scenes of seductions and random fights. Each section ends with the new character being knocked out, followed by their name crossed off a list, KILL BILL-style. The minutes tick away. We wonder what we're doing with our lives. Eventually, the cast wakes up in the sports arena from KICKBOXER 2 and are challenged by their captor Brick Bardo to compete in one-on-one fights to the death!

The in-ring combat doesn't have much flair, variation, or impact. They're one-note fights that repeat the same punch or kick from three to five different angles. Why? Probably because it adds pads out the running time! Fight choreographer Benny "The Jet" Urquidez may have been an essential part in delivering some of Jackie Chan's greatest one-on-one fights in WHEELS AND MEALS and DRAGONS FOREVER, but time was not on his side with on BLOODMATCH.

There's some exciting use of a spotlight to add visual flair to an empty set, but

we spend an hour in the arena, and it gets real old fast. Finally, things wrap up with the reveal that someone had plastic surgery (uh?) and the film finishes with a vague promise of a sequel. Okay.

I have a sneaking suspicion that BLOODMATCH came together because Pyun had the set of KICKBOXER 2 on hand for a weekend and thought to himself, "I made DECEIT

in three days! Why not do it again with a MATCH of BLOOD?" BLOODMATCH is slicker than DECEIT, as it has more variation in its storytelling (a steadicam makes an appearance!), but it's also pretty hollow. As you may have surmised, BLOODMATCH is not good. It has action, it has a plot, and eventually, it ends, but there's no passion behind any of it. Did Pyun simply want to challenge himself? To put Thom Mathews in a leading role? To make a little cash? Maybe it was done for all of those reasons, and that's fine, but I do feel bad for the suckers that pick it off the shelf, thinking it was a variation on BLOODSPORT, only to discover that it was really a sleep aid. From the high of KICKBOXER 2 to the lows of BLOODMATCH, Albert Pyun continued to prove himself an artist that loved to work, and work, and work, and work, and work and work, and work and work, and work and work.

55

DOLLMAN (1991)

CAST
Tim Thomerson, Jackie Earle Haley, Kamala Lopez

WRITER
Chris Roghair

PRODUCER
Cathy Gesualdo

CINEMATOGRAPHER
George Mooradian

MUSIC
Anthony Riparetti

PRODUCTION DESIGNER
Don Day

EDITOR
Margeret-Anne Smith

COSTUME DESIGN
Cindy Rosenthal

RUNTIME
79 mins

BACK OF THE BOX He's the toughest cop on planet Arturos. A fearless renegade. But when a high-speed space chase lands in the middle of a gang war in the Bronx, Brick Bardo (Tim Thomerson) is in a class all of his own: He's thirteen inches tall and armed with the deadliest weapon man has ever seen. As always, Brick has perfect timing: he lands just in time to save a streetwise woman from a scorching death at the hands of some of the drug thugs. She's Debi Alejandro (Kamala Lopez) and she's ruffled the feathers of the wrong group of people in her fight to clean up the neighbourhood. Debi takes Brick under her wing and he joins her crusade to eliminate drug lord Braxton Red (Jackie Earle Haley) Now Brick is known as a DOLLMAN... a criminal's deadliest nightmare.

IN CLASSIC Full Moon studio style, DOLLMAN was sold on the title, poster and nothing more. Initially conceived as a riff on THE INCREDIBLE SHRINKING MAN, Pyun redesigned it from the ground up as a noir take on the urban vigilantism of DEATH WISH III.

If you stumbled on DOLLMAN at 2:00 AM you'd probably assume it was a BLADE RUNNER rip-off along the lines of the Rutger Hauer vehicle SPLIT SECOND (1992). The film stars Tim Thomerson as a miniature Dirty Harry called Brick Bardo whose in the same wisecracking vein as Thomerson's Jack Death character from the TRANCERS series. It's only when Brick crash lands on earth while chasing the big bad (a floating head!) that we discover Bardo is nothing but a wee lad compared to the humans of earth. It's a good thing his gun can blow people up! Brick gets picked up by a local community organizer (Kamala Lopez), is taken to her apartment, and spends forty minutes sitting on her desk. Yeah, it's that kind of movie. The one surprise comes in the presence of Jackie Earl Haley

(WATCHMEN) who gives one hell of a committed performance as the local scenery chewing gang leader. As per usual for this period, Pyun's ace cinematographer George Mooradian covers everything in stylish smoke punctured by moody shafts of light.

DOLLMAN has a great opening and a fun finale. That's about it. It's a classic FULL MOON property: a great idea paired with a lukewarm execution that doesn't properly exploit its core concept. When interviewed for the great book on Full Moon Pictures, IT CAME FROM THE VIDEO AISLE, Pyun admitted he didn't remember much about making the film, and it isn't hard to see why. The picture spends the bulk of the running time in the same rubble-strewn location he would later use in NEMESIS. The rest of the running time takes place in a cramped apartment set that was built in the same warehouse where Pyun was shooting ARCADE. There's a germ of an idea in the moral (and literal) deconstruction of the fascist cop trope, with Kamala Lopez's pacifist character wanting Brick to step away from his violent ways, but it's way underdeveloped, and the final turn is head-scratching in its non-effectiveness. It's the kind of film where the hero can shoot a bad guy in the gut, blow off his arm and then be convinced "I guess it would be wrong to kill him now."

Pyun shot DOLLMAN and ARCADE for Full Moon back-to-back. It would be the second (and last) time he would work for Charles Band. I'm not sure what prompted Band to get in the Pyun business again after the disastrous experience of VICIOUS LIPS, but if I had to hazard a guess, it was probably because Pyun promised he could deliver two films for the price of one.

FUN FACT Dollman would reappear in the soul-crushing DOLLMAN VS DEMONIC TOYS (1993), but that was mostly stock footage from other Full Moon productions. Dollman's best iteration is in Full Moon's comic love letter to its fans: DOLLMAN KILLS THE FULL MOON UNIVERSE.

ARCADE (1991)

CAST
Megan Ward, Peter Billingsley, John de Lancie

WRITER
David S. Goyer

PRODUCER
Cathy Gesualdo

CINEMATOGRAPHER
George Mooradian

MUSIC
Alan Howarth

PRODUCTION DESIGNER
Don Day

EDITOR
Miles Wynton

COSTUME DESIGN
Cindy Rosenthal

RUNTIME
86 mins

BACK OF THE BOX There's a new video game at Dante's Inferno and the kids are dying to play it. It's Arcade, a new prototype with a life of its own, or rather that of a young tormented child. The game is guided by an organic microchip patterned after the boy's brainwaves and is an exciting adventure where the player enters the electronic world and becomes a part of the deadly game. One by one the players are starting to lose their minds and their lives, but when Alex (Megan Ward) loses her boyfriend she enlists the help of her friend Nick (Peter Billingsley) and together they decide to enter the game. They know that the odds are stacked against them, armed with only their wits and survival instincts, Alex and Nick enter Arcade for the final battle... just pray they make it home - Alive!

I SAW ARCADE AS A KID, AND IT SCARED THE BEJESUS OUTTA ME.

It was on one of the rare nights where I found myself alone in my dad's basement. I had rented ARCADE from the horror section. I knew it was going to be the scariest thing I had ever seen. Even more terrifying than GOOSEBUMPS books! I popped in the tape and held my breath. As it played out before my horrified eyes, ARCADE's weird pace and non-action perplexed me. I knew it looked cheap and nothing was happening, but by the time the final shot arrived (a small kid saying "Bitch" into the camera), I was shaking. The experience covered me in an itchy blanket of existential dread stitched out of pure irrationality. I recall running up the dark stairs propelled by a fear that the evil-sounding ARCADE could be right behind me. I had been struck by the power of cinema.

With that in mind, ARCADE is terrible.

The film follows a group of teens—including Full Moon mainstay Megan Ward, a pre-BUFFY Seth Green, and a post-A CHRISTMAS STORY Peter Billingsley—as they stumble onto a new VR game called ARCADE. The kids get sucked into the virtual world, and it's

up to Ward and Billingsley to "Kiss reality goodbye!" and save the day. Can our two clueless heroes defeat all the shitty CGI effects $750,000 can buy?

Made back to back with DOLLMAN, Full Moon's original pitch consisted of a bunch of teens being knocked off one by one in a haunted arcade, but things changed drastically when Pyun and screenwriter David Goyer came in with VR on the brain. The shooting draft of their script was supposedly insanely ambitious, and Pyun admits in the book IT CAME FROM THE VIDEO AISLE that he wasn't ready for the project's scope. He bailed from the production before it was finished and the producers (along with Peter Billingsley) were forced to step in, re-write most of the dialogue, and whip it into a releasable state. It didn't help that the production had to re-do all the special effects after Disney saw a trailer and noticed vehicles that looked suspiciously like the light-cycles from TRON.

It's easy to poke fun at the awful effects that make up the back-half of ARCADE. They're bad, there's no doubt about that, but the real sin is that they're boring. Each level features zero character interaction or decision-making, and the time in the game is mostly spent watching a first-person view of someone skateboarding down a castle hallway. Pulse pounding! It doesn't help that Pyun is way out of his depth and doesn't seem to have a clue on how to deliver horror-movie thrills. There are

no suspense sequences or gore gags anywhere in sight. There's probably a version of this story that plays like a slasher film, but this isn't it. Megan Ward wanders around aimlessly in the real world until the plot forces her to face off against the arcade. Once

she enters the game, it's like an episode of SECRETS OF THE CRYPTKEEPER'S HAUNTED HOUSE (yes, that existed) mixed in with a mediocre episode of ARE YOU AFRAID OF THE DARK? stretched out to 80 agonizing minutes. Its only merit is that it scared a young Justin Decloux (who should have known better).

NEMESIS (1992)

CAST
Olivier Gruner, Tim Thomerson, Cary-Hiroyuki Tagawa

WRITER
Rebecca Charles (Probably a pseudonym of Albert Pyun)

PRODUCERS
Tom Karnowski, Eric Karson, Ash R. Shah

CINEMATOGRAPHER
George Mooradian

MUSIC
Michel Rubini

PRODUCTION DESIGNER
E. Colleen Saro

EDITORS
Mark Conte, David Kern

COSTUME DESIGN
Lizz Wolf

RUNTIME
95 mins

BACK OF THE BOX — Los Angeles, 2027, Japan and America have merged politically and economically. Man and machines have merged as well. The scientific community has perfected cybernetics to the degree that any body part can be replaced. Nemesis is an action-packed sci-fi thriller where information is the ultimate power. System cowboys, information terrorists, bio-enhanced gangsters, and cyborg outlaws all play a part in this battle of man vs machine - in the future it pays to be more than human.

NEMESIS has all the things I love about Albert Pyun distilled to their purest forms: far-out sci-fi ideas, wild action scenes, and his burning passion for filmmaking. It's got all of Pyun's classic quirks as well: muddled pacing, an overcomplicated story, head-scratching editing choices, and a vision that's a little too ambitious for its reach — but damn, it sure comes close!

JCVD clone Olivier Gruner plays Alex Rain, a blade runn—sorry, cyborg hunter—who is introduced while being chased through a rubble-strewn wasteland where a jaw-dropping John Woo-style gun battle erupts. For the first time in his career, it feels like Pyun has everything lined up to pull off his vision: a unique location, brave stuntmen, and fiery pyrotechnics all come together to deliver one hell of a thrilling action scene that ends with Olivier being blown up (while saving a dog!). He's rebuilt as a cyborg and forced by two government agents (Tim Thomerson and Brion James) to take out a terrorist in the ghost town of Shang-Lu. Of course, nothing is at it seems, and the film turns into Pyun's version of Dashiell Hammett's RED HARVEST. The shit hits the fan, and Gruner is propelled into a lengthy gunfight/chase that jumps from Hong Kong-style action to vine-swinging jungle adventure without batting an eye.

The project's inception had the usual Pyun origins: he originally wanted to do something completely different. The first iteration of the story was supposed to star a 12-year-old girl. Pyun had 22-year-old Megan Ward in mind, but when he sold his script to Imperial

Entertainment, the company behind ventures like DOUBLE DRAGON and Van Damme's LIONHEART, and they requested/demanded he make their new prospect Olivier Gruner the star. I assume in the original version a male action star would have been blown up in the first battle and be replaced GHOST IN THE SHELL-style by Megan Ward for the rest of the picture — but beyond that, there are not many traces of how it would have been different. In the re-written role, Olivier Gruner does his admirable best. His incredible physique matched with his heavily accented English dialogue results in a deadpan protagonist that never quite feels human. Perfect, really. It also helps that Gruner gets to bounce off an all-star cast of Pyun regulars that include Tim Thomerson, Brion James (sporting another terrible accent), Cary-Hiroyuki Tagawa, and lucky charm Thom Mathews. Plus, there's a bevy of powerful women that include Merle Kennedy, Marjorie Monaghan and Deborah Shelton who fearlessly spends most of her role fully nude.

Every time I watch NEMESIS I wonder why it works so well and so many other Pyun films falter. Was it some indescribable alchemical energy? Merely a money issue? Did Imperial give him more creative leeway? Or was it merely the right talent coming together at the right time? NEMESIS has Pyun's trademark shaky storytelling, but I'd argue that most of his decisions pay off in a satisfying fashion. It's so dense that only on the third re-watch did I realize a character had switched bodies with a major villain! The production is also helped immensely by the impressive practical effects by David and Michelle Barton, the manic stunts coordinated by veteran Roddie Rondell Jr., and some very confident cinematography by workhorse George Mooradian. The steadicam work by Mark Emery Moore (who went on to be one of the best operators in the business) is particularly impressive. It makes sense that the original NEMESIS would launch a series, but it's a bummer the sequels were so disconnected plot-wise and saddled with microscopic budgets. Perhaps Pyun's curse is that he would often be forced to build roller coasters without any dips (special effects), banks (stunts), or flips (technical equipment). With NEMESIS, we see what could have been.

FUN FACT Pyun's original script for NEMESIS was supposed to be the last film of his three-picture deal with Cannon Films after DOWN TWISTED and DANGEROUSLY CLOSE. They wanted him to make a more "mainstream action movie" (ha!). In its original conception, the film was called ALEX RAIN and was more of a serial killer procedural with cyberpunk elements. The first draft was shelved when Cannon went bust along with a Pyun remake of JOHNNY GUITAR that was meant to star John Travolta!

DOUBLE FUN FACT I've screened NEMESIS twice on 35mm, and the first time Albert Pyun was kind enough to send a video intro answering a handful of questions. He made one assertion that has always mystified me: he'd spend the first few days of every shoot filming random inserts with no clear guide of how to include them in the movie. He called it "Rock 'N' Roll Filmmaking," and it angered the producers to no end.

TRIPLE FUN FACT Yes, that is a naked Thomas Jane being choked out by Deborah Shelton.

KNIGHTS (1992)

CAST
Kathy Long, Kris Kristofferson, Lance Henriksen

WRITER
Albert Pyun

PRODUCER
Tom Karnowski

CINEMATOGRAPHER
George Mooradian

MUSIC
Anthony Riparetti

PRODUCTION DESIGNER
Phil Zarling

EDITORS
Dean Goodhill

COSTUME DESIGN
Lizz Wolf

RUNTIME
90 mins

BACK OF THE BOX In the ravaged wasteland of the future, mankind is terrorized by cyborgs - robots with human features - that have discovered a new source of fuel: human blood. Commanded by their vicious leader Job (Lance Henriksen, Jennifer Eight) the cyborgs prepare to overtake Taos, a densely populated human outpost. Only one force can stop Joe's death march - the cyborg Gabriel (Kris Kristofferson) who is programmed to destroy Job and his army. In the ruins of a ransacked village, Gabriel finds Nea (Kathy Long) a beautiful young woman whose parents were killed by the cyborgs ten years earlier. Now she wants revenge. They strike a pact: Gabriel will train Nea to fight the cyborgs, and Nea will lead Gabriel to Taos. Five-time kickboxing champion Kathy Long has all the right moves in this high-speed adventure that delivers plenty of action.

> "LET ME DIE MY DEATH. I HAVE NEVER EXPERIENCED THE PAIN OF BIRTH. THERE YOU ARE, WRAP ME IN YOUR WINGS, LIKE A BLACK PARROT."
>
> *- Robot Vampire (Lance Henriksen)*

Pyun made a wuxia for the American direct-to-video market. Of course, everyone hated it.

For the unfamiliar, the term Wuxia is used to denote the Chinese "flying swordsman" genre and is a blanket term (literally translating to "martial heroes") to describe stories that feature roaming martial arts warriors who fight with fantastic physical techniques. The heroes and villains of these tales can spin a sword on a finger, jump hundreds of feet in the air, and blow up an opponent by hitting specific pressure points. One of the leading 20th-century innovators of the genre was author Jin Yong (under the pen name Louis Cha) who wrote the mega-popular newspaper serial THE LEGEND OF THE CONDOR HEROES. Film classics of the genre include King Hu's A TOUCH OF ZEN (1971), Chor Yuen's THE MAGIC BLADE (1976), Ching Siu-Tung's DUEL TO THE DEATH (1983), and

Tsui Hark's ZU: WARRIORS FROM THE MAGIC MOUNTAIN (1983). The wuxia continues to remain popular in Asia to this day.

The English speaking world has been bred to accept super-heroes, but flying swordsmen have always been one step too far. Most films that tackle wuxia style action find ways to explain it (they're in THE MATRIX, so wire-work is okay!) or say something like "they can jump so high because they're cyborgs!"

And so, we've come back around to Pyun's KNIGHTS.

In the desert of a post-apocalyptic future, a group of blood drinking cyborgs (led by Lance Henriksen) ransack a village and leave Kathy Long (a real-life kickboxer) as the only survivor. She witnesses a mysterious man named Gabriel (Kris Kristofferson and his hard-working stunt double) kill one of the robot baddies in a balletic battle on the edge of a cliff, so she asks Gabriel (who reveals himself to be a cyborg as well) to take her on as a student to learn the ways of metal murder. They team up and vow to stop the evil cyborgs before they reach an outpost to chow down on the last 10,000 humans.

Wuxia signifiers are all over KNIGHTS. There are wandering swordsmen, the calling-out of fight techniques, and the film's overall stylistic construction. Pyun has mentioned in interviews that two of his favourite filmmakers are Tsui Hark and King Hu, and it's never more evident than in KNIGHTS. He captures all the fights with big wide-angle lenses (à la Hark), combatants jump off-screen to re-appear a mile away (à la Hu), and gravity is a mere obstacle to overcome. That type of stylistic action would not come to America until the art-house veneer of CROUCHING TIGER, HIDDEN DRAGON (2000) made it mainstream (which was only doable thanks to the popularity of THE MATRIX having opened the back door). At a different time, perhaps Pyun's noble efforts with KNIGHTS would have been rewarded instead of resoundingly mocked. I vividly remember years ago reading reviews of KNIGHTS where the author compared Pyun's film making to Ed Wood (which is objectively untrue). The difference between stylistic choices and missed opportunities may be a thin one at times in Pyun's cash-strapped oeuvre, but in KNIGHTS it's reasonably clear Pyun was in total control.

To be fair, it doesn't help that Pyun is much more interested in unique performers instead of believable ones. Real-life kickboxer Kathy Long has a fantastic look that echoes Linda Hamilton in the first TERMINATOR, but delivering dialogue is not her strong suits. Lance Henriksen, as the leader of cyborgs, goes full ham with a giant rubber robot arm and tendency to drool uncontrollably. Kris Kristofferson is his usual gruff self as Long's mechanical mentor. The rest of the cast is filled out with Pyun regulars like Gary Daniels (a personal favourite) and Nicholas Guest as a wise-cracking henchman. The special effects by the always-reliable Dave Barton give the fight scenes a gory punch (flaming robots heads!).

Before you race out to buy KNIGHTS on a VHS, I have to admit I'm rating it on a steep curve. I know it can't hold a candle to the cinema that inspired it. The combat is much slower and the editing way sloppier, but Pyun is trying to do something no one had really attempted in America, and that's what I find so damn endearing. The desert landscapes give it a wide-open feel that is often absent from his work. The endlessly clever gags pulled off by the stunt team (which include future JOHN WICK director Chad Stahelski) are still impressive in their absurdity. The epic 20-minute finale has Kathy Long fighting dozens of baddies as she races across a dusty mountain, kicking and moving like lightning. At one point she straps a cut-in-half Kristofferson (whose still alive) to her back and they both fight with swords simultaneously thanks to a mix of little person double and stunt dummy. It's the kind of wild physicality you rarely got to see in 90s action cinema.

The film's arid location and focus on edged weapons is reminiscent of Tsui Hark's THE BLADE, and I would have assumed Hark's masterpiece heavily inspired Pyun… if it wasn't for the fact that THE BLADE came out two years later.

Great minds think alike!

FUN FACT   FUN FACT Pyun had conceived KNIGHTS as CYBORG 2, but when the production company that owned the rights decided to go in another direction (which resulted in CYBORG 2: GLASS SHADOW starring Angelina Jolie), Pyun chose to move forward with his concept anyway. In honesty, it has very little do with the JCVD original beyond the fact that there are so-called cyborgs and it takes place in a ruined future. The real pleasures of KNIGHTS come from its stripped-down efficiency. Pyun tried to deliver a form of action storytelling that didn't exist in the cinematic language of the casual video store renter, and for that, the film was doomed to fail. KNIGHTS would be the last time for a while that Pyun would try such a bold experiment

BRAIN SMASHER... A LOVE STORY (1993)

CAST
Andrew Dice Clay, Teri Hatcher, Yuji Okumoto

WRITER
Albert Pyun

PRODUCER
Tom Karnowski

CINEMATOGRAPHER
George Mooradian

MUSIC
Anthony Riparetti

PRODUCTION DESIGNER
Phil Zarling

EDITOR
Lauren A. Schaffer

COSTUME DESIGN
Meta Jardine

RUNTIME
98 mins

BACK OF THE BOX He's Rambo, Superman and The Terminator all rolled into one muscle-bound fighting machine. He never backs down and he eats bullies for breakfast. He's strong, he's brave, he's invincible. He's the bouncer with attitude, the toughest guy in town, with a hard head and a soft heart - especially for beautiful young models in distress. He's Ed Malloy - The Brain Smasher! This raucous outrageous action comedy stars America's hottest young comedian (Andrew Dice Clay) star of 'The Adventures of Ford Fairlane' and the gorgeous Teri Hatcher (from 'Soapdish') outwitting, outfight and outrunning a gang of deadly Chinese ninjas in a thrill-a-minute story that will delight fans of wild adventure movies like 'Big Trouble in Little China'. Gasp in amazement as the Neanderthal Brain Smasher keeps the peace while leaving his enemies in pieces. Laugh out loud at his feeble attempts to seduce the air head model while trying to save the world the ultimate weapon of destruction - a tiny red flower! The Brain Smasher... it's mind blowing.

FOR A BRIEF MOMENT Andrew Dice Clay was the biggest stand-up comic in the world. Everyone knew his name. He sold out Madison Square Garden multiple nights in a row. He starred in the major motion picture THE ADVENTURES OF FORD FAIRLANE (1990), produced by Joel Silver.

His fall was quick. Three years later, he was in a film directed by Albert Pyun.

Professional model Sam Crain (Teri Hatcher) is asked by her sister to smuggle a flower that grants immortality, but when the trade-off goes wrong, Sam finds herself on the run through the night chased by a gang of Shaolin monks ("We're not ninjas!") in the city of Portland. She bumps into a bouncer named Brainsmasher (Andrew Dice Clay), who is too much of a nice guy to let her get into trouble, so he tags along to make sure she survives till daybreak.

It's a challenge to consider BRAINSMASHER...A LOVE STORY as anything more than a joke. The silly title! It stars Andrew "Diceman" Clay! It was slated for theatrical release and then dumped to video! That must mean it sucks, right? I don't remember what prompted me to check out the film almost a decade ago (very early on in my Pyun odyssey), but I distinctly remember being taken aback. It was fun! It had a sense of scope and style! The Diceman was charming!?

If I had been aware of Andrew Dice Clay in his prime, I'm sure I would still hate him with a fiery passion. He didn't tell jokes. Instead, he spouted off the most sexist, racist and "Un-PC" things he could think up. And if someone cried foul (as many did), he'd deflect the criticism by saying his act was just a "character" and that he wasn't a hateful person at all. His fans didn't care. They simply loved that someone was saying all the toxic things they were thinking.

With that in mind, the reality is that Andrew Clay (as he likes to be billed on screen) is a pretty good actor, especially after his fame had receded. Once the Diceman character was banished from the mainstream, Clay just became another burly dude whose best years were behind him. There's a sadness to his presence, and BRAINSMASHER understands how to exploit it. The Brainsmasher character lives with his parents, and while he knows he isn't one of the smartest guys in the room, he'll always jump to someone's defence.

Teri Hatcher as his co-star is a perfect comedic foil, a fast-talking beauty that doesn't put up with any of his shit. It helps that the film's one-night premise forces Pyun to tell a linear story. The larger budget also allows cinematographer George Mooradian to bring a more significant scope to the visuals, with Portland captured in beautiful wides filled with reflective slicked down streets.

The script tends to hit the same jokes over and over again like "We're not ninjas. We're Shaolin monks," the bad guys scream about a hundred times, or "I'm a model, but I'm not an airhead," Terri Hatcher continually quips. It's like the film wants to put its thesis in bright, bold lights: People are not necessarily who they appear to be on the surface. Andrew Dice Clay can't be all bad, right?

BRAIN SMASHER is an amusing and stylish action comedy with a charming pair of leads and a swift pace. I wonder if Albert Pyun could have moved to greener pastures if the film had come out and been a mild success?

I guess we'll never know.

FUN FACT Andrew Dice Clay's self-awareness is pretty debatable, but it's undeniable that his stand-up album THE DAY THE LAUGHTER DIED is one for the books. It's a double album that chronicles a show Clay did in a small comedy club around the peak of his fame. It's a tortuous set that devolves into Clay verbally attacking everyone in the audience. Not only was it produced by Rick Rubin, but it was released to the public at large and went gold! He even made a sequel that ends with him getting into a fight.

DOUBLE FUN FACT For a long time, Andrew Dice Clay continued to try to do his thing to little acclaim. He did a few low-budget acting gigs, like the villain in Paul Lynch's NO CONTEST (as Andrew Clay), but he was entirely off the radar until the ENTOURAGE TV show granted him a second life. His re-appraisal got him a role in Woody Allen's BLUE JASMINE, he appeared in the Martin Scorsese directed pilot for the series VINYL, and he even had a CURB YOUR ENTHUSIASM-style show called DICE that lasted for two seasons. In 2018, he had a significant role in Bradley Cooper's multiple Oscar-nominated A STAR IS BORN (and he was great in it). I would have bet a few years ago that Clay would probably turn into a full-time Joe Piscopo-style right-wing personality, but it hasn't happened yet. off to whoever is keeping him in check!

KICKBOXER 4: THE AGGRESSOR (1994)

CAST
Sasha Mitchell, Kamel Krifa, Brad Thornton

WRITERS
David Yorkin, Albert Pyun

PRODUCER
Jessica G. Budin

CINEMATOGRAPHER
George Mooradian

MUSIC
Anthony Riparetti

PRODUCTION DESIGNER
Timothy Gordon

EDITOR
Ken Morrisey

COSTUME DESIGN
Shelly Busalacchi

RUNTIME
86 mins

BACK OF THE BOX Sasha Mitchell ("Kickboxer 2&3") triumphantly returns to the ring as David Sloan, fighting not just for his survival, but for his beautiful wife, who has become the sexual captive of the despicable world champion, Tong Po. Framed, forgotten and furious, Sloan has been wasting away in prison, but the Feds agree to release him, if he will lead them inside Po's impenetrable Mexican fortress, protected by its deadly guards and adorned by its sexual slaves. Sloan reluctantly teams up with a female fighter to gain entry into Po's tournament of champions, a savage battle where winner takes all - and to Sloan - that means everything.

IN THE SECOND KICKBOXER, we had the meditative story of David Sloan (Sasha Mitchell) trying to move on with his life. In the third KICKBOXER (directed by Rick King), the kickboxing action was ditched in favour of a gun wielding Sloan and his master (Denis Chan) taking on a ring of white slavers. In the fourth entry, Pyun returned to the director's chair. This time around, David Sloan is a burnt out fighter who is stuck in prison after being framed for murder by the annoyingly persistent Tong Po, who also kidnapped Sloan's wife. A viewer could safely assume the kidnapping and imprisonment happened in the last movie, but they would be wrong. KICKBOXER 4 is a sequel to a film that never existed.

As you can tell, Pyun is on an entirely different tonal wavelength than his previous KICKBOXER outing, and in my opinion, it's not a comfortable fit. He's got the same technical crew, but it feels like everyone's on autopilot. The entire production has a laissez-faire attitude that is only magnified by the fact that the deadly underground tournament takes place at Tong Po's Relaxation Ranch. Sasha Mitchell has fun with the burnt-out anti-hero nature of this

iteration of David Sloan, but for some reason (scheduling conflicts?) the story veers off of him halfway through to follow another fighter (who's a bit of a snooze) played by Brad Thornton. The story also has a weird sexist undercurrent, with all the women characters being bad fighters who need to be saved. All of these bits don't make the film terrible, but they do make it forgettable, which is disappointing compared to Pyun's previous work in the franchise. Pyun does have fun with the fact that JCVD's pal Kamel Krifa plays Tong Po. The film takes every opportunity to portray the ruthless Thai fighter as a chatterbox (and successful record producer?) with a gentle Belgian accent.

The one highlight of the picture is an early fight in which Mitchell takes on a bunch of random goons in a bar. The set-piece is perfectly paced, features a dozen creative stunts, and some great comedic punchlines. Perhaps Pyun spent too much time on the bar fight and was forced to rush through the rest of the script to arrive on time and on budget?

FUN FACT There would be further films in KICKBOXER series, but Sasha Mitchell would not return. KICKBOXER 5 stars Mark Dacascos as a friend of the Sloan family, and the long-gap sequel KICKBOXER: VENGEANCE (2016) would be a remake of the original that led into KICKBOXER: RETALIATION (2018) and KICKBOXER: ARMAGEDDON (2020).

HONG KONG '97 (1994)

CAST
Robert Patrick, Brion James, Tim Thomerson

WRITER
Randall Fontana

PRODUCERS
Tom Karnowski, Gary Schmoeller

CINEMATOGRAPHER
George Mooradian

MUSIC
Michael McCarty

PRODUCTION DESIGNERS
Rodell Cruz,
Rosa Pang

EDITOR
Ken Morrisey

COSTUME DESIGN
Shelly Busalacchi

RUNTIME
86 mins

BACK OF THE BOX At one past midnight, July 1, 1997 Great Britain's lease on the Territory of Hong Kong will expire and The People's Republic of China will be the new rulers. Reg Cameron (Robert Patrick) is a deadly corporate assassin who receives orders to eliminate a high ranking mainland China General on the eve of the Hong Kong's reversion to China. After he assassinates the General with his trademark twin beretta 9mm's, he finds out that the orders were given by his bosses to set him up. With a $10,000,000 bounty on his head, Reg must race against the clock to escape from Hong Kong before midnight reversion to China. However, his exist against insurmountable odds as the Red Army, Triad Gunmen and his own bosses who have set him up are on his track. The action is non-stop as Reg seeks the assistance of his mentor and fellow hitman Simon Alexander (Brion James), his buddy Jack McGraw (Tim Thomerson) and his ex-girlfriend Kate (Min-Na Wen) in order to flee Hong Kong with his life.

IT MUST HAVE BEEN difficult to fathom how Hong Kong would be impacted when it switched from British to Chinese rule in 1997. Britain's imperialist occupation of Hong Kong was a terrible thing, but the populace had constructed their lives around it, and they were now forced to reckon with a massive change to their everyday existence — one that was going to include a lot less freedom and a lot more government oversight. Hundreds of films examined the oncoming handover, subtly in Tsui Hark's GREEN SNAKE (1993) and Wong Kar-wai's HAPPY TOGETHER (1997), and head-on in Herman Yau's FROM THE QUEEN TO THE CHIEF EXECUTIVE (2001). They are all great works of art. HONG KONG '97 is not one of them.

Robert Patrick (the T-1000 himself) wanders the crowded streets of Hong Kong in a giant coat. In slow motion. He enters a bar and shoots someone THE KILLER-style. In slow motion. He makes sweet love to a woman in a room illuminated by expressionist coloured backdrops straight out of THE BRIDE WITH WHITE HAIR — in slow motion. Assassins burst through the windows — in slow motion. Robert Patrick, buck naked, grabs his weapons and blows them away — in slow motion. Uh-Oh. That's a lot of slow motion.

Robert Patrick kills the wrong guy, someone puts a hit on him, and he teams up with Pyun stock players Tim Thomerson and Brion James (sporting his patented all-over-the-place British accent) to escape Hong Kong.

They can't, so they jog in place until the running time hits that magic feature-length number. Patrick's old flame

shows up (played by AGENTS OF SHIELD and ER star Ming-Na Wen), and they bicker a little. Robert Patrick wears a suit that makes him look like he's play acting in his father's clothes. The film is shot on a floating steadicam with little direction. The dialogue is often muffled to the point of incomprehension. Exteriors look like they were grabbed guerrilla-style without a permit (which is cool). It's the kind of project that hangs on by a thread. There's no passion to be found, just adequate competence with a beginning, middle and end.

There is something undeniably appealing about a hero wielding hot death in both hands as he blasts away an army of nameless villains in suits. Everyone wants to stage gunfights like John Woo, and the iconography seems easy: Get two pistols, a cool-as-cucumber protagonist, and tons of slow motion. The problem is that filmmakers think that merely putting all those elements together constitutes a good action scene, when in reality, it just highlights how much of a master Woo was in making it art. Albert Pyun has the iconography down pat in HONG KONG '97, but he fails to implement any understandable geography, exciting physicality, or the mix of film speeds that are essential to turn a gunfight into a bullet ballet. Here, it's just dull characters firing at each other in slow motion. Endless slow motion.

Pyun has nailed Woo-ish action in the past with NEMESIS, so it's extra frustrating that it feels so phoned in here. Every gunfight plays like a half-remembered thought, never exciting or engaging, destined to be forgotten as white noise. Pyun tries to make up for the lack of content by dumping on the profanity and gratuitous female nudity, but it only magnifies the hollowness of the entire enterprise.

FUN FACT There's a terrible video game called HONG KONG '97 about a relative of Bruce Lee trying to save the world from an evil army. This film has nothing to do with it.

SPITFIRE (1995)

CAST
Debra Jo Fondren, Sarah Douglas, Lance Henriksen

WRITERS
Albert Pyun, David Yorkin, Christopher Borkgren

PRODUCERS
Tom Karnowski, Gary Schmoeller

CINEMATOGRAPHER
George Mooradian

MUSIC
Anthony Riparetti

PRODUCTION DESIGNERS
Rodell Cruz, Rosa Pang

EDITOR
Dennis M. O'Connor

COSTUME DESIGN
Shelly Busalacchi

RUNTIME
95 mins

BACK OF THE BOX Beautiful and gifted, Charlie Case is a star gymnast and martial arts expert. But when her mother is brutally murdered and her father kidnapped, Charlie suddenly finds herself drawn into the nightmare world of organized crime and counter-espionage. An international crime cartel, convinced that Charlie knows the whereabouts of a disk containing a nuclear weapon's launch codes, unleashes renegade CIA operative Carla Davis to track her down. Never more than one step ahead of Carla and her ruthless gang of henchmen, Charlie will need every kick and trick in the book if she's going to live long enough to save her father... and pull the world back from the brink of destruction.

SPITFIRE is the kind of lighthearted romp Pyun was rarely able to pull off. The reality is that most of his films ended up as tortured husks of their original intentions that barely crawled across the finish line. Not so, here! He obviously has a little money to work with, a great roster of charming character actors, and a breezy globe-trotting adventure to hang it all on.

Lance Henriksen opens the film as a James Bond-ish spy who gets caught in the act of naked mambo by a former flame. The flame/rival spy (Sarah Douglas) demands that Lance give her some nuclear codes, but when Lance refuses, a shootout breaks out, and he escapes with a jet pack. Fun! We then follow the film's actual protagonist, a gymnast named Charlie Case, played by real-life gymnast Kristie Phillips in her first (and last) feature film role. She's in the middle of a world tour when she comes into possession of the much-sought-after nuclear codes, and learns that she is one of the illegitimate children of Lance's super spy. But most importantly, will Charlie arrive in time to compete in the gymnastics world championships against the evil Russian team!?

The baddies give chase and Phillips is thrown into a CHARADE-style romp through the Bahamas, Athens, Rome and Hong Kong, where she is met in every new locale by another illegitimate child of her super-spy father. James Bond types should really use protection! Tim Thomerson, in a hilarious Andy Warhol haircut, co-stars as Charlie's goofball companion.

Pyun's female-fronted version of GYMKATA is content in playing out like a comedic travelogue through a bunch of exotic locations. It's the kind of film where a lot of time is spent in hotels. The scenes set on the neon-lit streets of Hong Kong are particularly impressive when you consider Pyun is shooting it all guerrilla-style without a permit.

Kristie Phillips as the film's lead is not much of an actor, but she does have a fiery presence that charmingly pairs with her thick southern accent and impressive cartwheeling skills. Her handful of action scenes are amusing, but I wish there were more of them. The standout set-piece is a chase across a dozen boats in Hong Kong that is punctuated by one of the funniest shots in Pyun's filmography. Sandra Douglas (of SUPERMAN the movie fame) gives it her all as the frustrated baddie who wants to get it all over with, while Thomerson does his best pathetic sidekick shtick.

SPITFIRE is the kind of picture you would stumble upon while channel surfing on a lazy Sunday afternoon. It's frivolous and weightless, but I'd rather watch the tiny Kristie Phillips try to act like a badass in a leather jacket then hear GYMKATA's Kurt Thomas whine like a baby.

FUN FACT This was shot right after HONG KONG '97 and the stars of that film, Robert Patrick and Brion James, show up briefly as goons in the opening shootout, where Patrick's arm is lit on fire!

DOUBLE FUN FACT The score by Tony Riparetti recycles his songs SHE'S ON FIRE and TURN AWAY from RADIOACTIVE DREAMS in vocal and instrumental form.

HEATSEEKER (1995)

CAST
Keith Cooke, Tina Cote, Norbert Weisser

WRITERS
Albert Pyun, Christopher Borkgren

PRODUCERS
Tom Karnowski, Gary Schmoeller

CINEMATOGRAPHER George Mooradian	**MUSIC** Anthony Riparetti	**PRODUCTION DESIGNER** Rodell Cruz
EDITOR Ken Morrisey	**COSTUME DESIGN** Shelly Busalacchi	**RUNTIME** 91 mins

BACK OF THE BOX In the year 2019 in New America. In the violent arena of unarmed combat one man is undisputed champion - Chance O'Brien - the only 100% human fighter in a sport dominated by cyborgs. But O'Brien's days may be numbered. Xao (Gary Daniels) is the ultimate warrior; a bio-enhanced fighting machine developed by a sinister corporation to prove to the world, once and for all, that mere flesh and blood are no match for their awesome technology. Challenged to take part in a clash of martial arts titans, O'Brien at first refuses, but when his girlfriend (Tina Cote) is held ransom he knows he has to fight... and win. In a series of brutal confrontation he uses all his skills to dispose of his opponents one by one before the final showdown — the invincible Chance O'Brien versus the indestructible cyborg Xao in a fight to the finish.

HEATSEEKER is a straight-down-the-middle Pyun outing. Not bad. Not great. It's a better tournament film then KICKBOXER 4, and it moves along at a nice clip, but it never pushes things far enough. The story follows a top-of-his-game kickboxer named Chance O'Brien (the charming Keith Cooke) who is forced to enter a deadly tournament to save his coach and fiancée (Tina Coté). It's a cookie-cutter premise, but it offers exciting action because all the fighters are supposed to be "enhanced," except for our hero. Unfortunately, all the cyborgs are the same shirtless dudes in gym shorts that plagued '90s martial arts cinema, and Chance quickly takes down every upgraded opponent without breaking a sweat. The only visual indication we get that the fighters are cyborgs happens when they get damaged, and the camera lingers on their destroyed bodies — which allows the ever-reliable Dave Baton to show off some nifty practical gore.

A distancing effect comes into play during the action scenes because Pyun is starting to use his "Shoot it all on a long lens!" time saving style. All the fights take place in a large arena, so Pyun pre-lit the set, put multiple cameras around the ring and had the fighters perform the choreography in one straight go. The final edit makes the action play out like a sports game which robs it of any impact. There's a glimmer of exciting story development when we learn that the baddies (led by the reigning King of Pyun Players, Norbert Weisser) have kidnapped Chance's coach/fiancée to force her to train the big bad Xao (the great Gary Daniels), but most importantly, fall in love with him, because love is more potent than any enhancements! It's a clever conceit, and there's a sense that it's going to throw a wrench in the black and white proceedings, but the film never gives Xao enough development, so when the finale happens we don't care that he loses (which he does, of course). Thom Mathews shows up as a good guy, who is obviously a baddie, but then turns back to good! A nice change of pace.

ON THE MATTER OF CYBORGS

When people think of Albert Pyun, they assume his filmography is mostly made up of robots fighting in martial arts tournaments. But is that true? First, there was CYBORG (1989), his Cannon film with Van "The Man" Damage. It's right there in the title, even though the cyborg is a minor character.

Secondly, there was NEMESIS (1992). Pyun's original idea was to have the lead role be played by a 12-year-old girl who would act like a typical macho action hero. The distributor pooh-poohed Pyun's idea and saddled him with a JCVD clone instead.

Thirdly, there's KNIGHTS (1993), which was meant to be a sequel to CYBORG (but you'd never know). The "enhanced human idea" is mostly a gateway to cool practical effects and crazy Hong Kong-style acrobatics.

Fourth, you have the three sequels to NEMESIS (95-96). The first two were shot back to back, and the third was shot in a few days to give Pyun something to do during pick-ups on ADRENALIN: FEAR THE RUSH. The sequels have almost nothing to do with the original and are mostly an excuse for Pyun to showcase his love of William Gibson cyberpunk aesthetics and woman bodybuilders.

Then there's HEATSEEKER (1995), which used the cyborgs as window dressing, and OMEGA DOOM (1996), where the nature of the broken down cyborgs allowed Pyun to tell a minimalist tale.

In a career that encompasses 44 films, Pyun has made eight cyborg-centric pictures, which is about 18% of his output. A recurring theme? Sure, but I would not call it an obsession. When questioned about his penchant for returning to the enhanced heroes, Pyun would often shrug and say, "I guess the storytelling possibilities of what it means to be a human being was interesting?" — but what he means is, "I made one movie that was a success and people gave me money to make other ones like it."

FUN FACT I assume Pyun is going to return to cyborgs in INTERSTELLAR CIVIL WAR: SHADOWS OF THE EMPIRE and NEMESIS: DARK RIFT, but they haven't been released yet, and the latter may still be a pipe dream along with KICKBOXER: ALGIERS and KICKBOXER: CITY OF BLOOD.

NEMESIS 2: NEBULA (1995)

CAST
Sue Price, Chad Stahelski, Tina Cote

WRITER
Albert Pyun

PRODUCERS
Tom Karnowski, Gary Schmoeller

CINEMATOGRAPHER
George Mooradian

MUSIC
Anthony Riparetti

PRODUCTION DESIGNERS
Rob Bowen,
Tracy Hennigan

EDITOR
Ken Morrisey

COSTUME DESIGN
Shelly Busalacchi

RUNTIME
83 mins

BACK OF THE BOX A deadly hunt that spans centuries is underway. A self-repairing, bio-tech giant Nebula Cyborg has found its target - Alex - a human created with super human DNA and hidden as a child in the East African Wasteland in the latter 20th century. Alex, who carries the future of mankind, is forced to flee at a ballistic pace through a raging civil war and mercenaries. She is relentlessly pursued by the awesome power of the Nebula as it zeros in on its deadly prey. UN soldiers meet fire power with more fire power to end Cyborg rule, but Alex can't hide in the 20th century forever. The race for humankind is on and the future just got darker.

NEMESIS 2 often gets dismissed because it isn't anything like the original, but once you get past the interminable flashback filled opening, it's actually an entertaining chase film. Albert Pyun said he wanted to model it after THE NAKED PREY (1965) which is a lean and mean picture where Cornel Wilde is hunted down in the African desert. Just like its inspiration, NEMESIS 2 is set in the sand and keeps the dialogue to a minimum. The new Alex (Sue Price) is not a trained actor, but it's refreshing to see a woman bodybuilder at the center of an action film, and she's got a rough-edged charm.

In a classic Poverty Row filmmaking move, Pyun said he made a conscious decision to keep the camera on a tripod and rarely move it. He makes it work. The static shooting style helped him get 100 set-ups a day and allowed him to inject a montage based energy to the film's set-pieces. Sure, there's no Olivier Gruner, and the John Woo-style action is absent, but it still has a propulsive energy all of its own.

It's interesting to consider that Albert Pyun's tireless drive to make movies is the single thing that kept him in the business, but also made it impossible for him to jump to the big leagues. Maybe it could have happened around the time of CAPTAIN AMERICA (if it had received a proper budget), with the theatrical release of KICKBOXER 2, or the video success of the original NEMESIS, or... Honestly, I don't think it could have ever happened.

That's not how Albert Pyun approached the work!

His body had to be in constant motion, so he took on more and more projects until his name was synonymous with direct-to-video pictures with cyborgs on the cover. By then, it was too late. No big studio would touch him. Even when the distributor gave Albert the simple task of making a straight sequel to NEMESIS, he couldn't help himself from shooting something entirely different instead. NEMESIS 2 is a fun movie, but its style is so different from the first that it probably alienated a lot of its audience.

Pyun couldn't allow himself to get bored with the work that he was doing. Like a shark, if he stopped moving, he would die. Pyun was the '90s DTV action equivalent of Spanish Writer/Director Jess Franco — who also couldn't stop working — and that meant he never gave all his films the attention they needed. Pyun released three films in 1995 and a jaw-dropping five in 1996. It's the work of someone so strongly driven by a need to create that it can only lead to self-destruction.

A HYPOTHESIS...

In my opinion, Pyun never got the fan base he deserved for two significant reasons: 1. There's no major genre community for action films like there is for horror. 2. His films never played in syndication on television like the 50s and 60s science fiction films which fostered an entire generation of Monster Kids.

THE DIRECTOR'S CUTS

Albert Pyun has said the bulk of his films were taken out of his hands and meddled with by producers before being released to the public. In an attempt to salvage his original visions, Pyun started to self-distribute "Director's Cuts" of his earlier pictures on DVD around 2013. I love that they exist, but there are a few factors that make it difficult for me to evaluate them critically. I won't be discussing any of them in detail in this book except for CYBORG, because it's the most famous of the mutilations.

Firstly, the Director's Cuts had to be bought directly from Albert, and that window has closed, which means that they're now incredibly difficult to procure.

Secondly, I'm not sure how many Director's Cuts were released. His website once listed a whopping nine upcoming releases, including a tantalizing RADIOACTIVE DREAMS Director's Cut, but that page has since been taken down.

Thirdly, the Director's Cuts are sourced from deteriorating VHS tapes, which often results a in fuzzy audio and visual presentation. It gets even muddier when you consider that most of these workprints weren't even close to being complete, so Pyun went in and made further changes to the films before releasing them on DVD which included adding title cards, sound effects and music that are often very clumsily integrated into the final product.

The Director's Cut DVD releases were 2-disc sets with one disc featuring the movie and the second disc featuring the film with an Albert Pyun commentary track. The commentary tracks are essential listening to anyone interested in Pyun's process. He's honest, full of praise, and very critical of a lot of his decisions.

To my knowledge, the following films were released as Director's Cuts:

- KNIGHTS (as KINGDOM OF METAL)
- MEAN GUNS
- ADRENALIN: FEAR THE RUSH
- CYBORG (as SLINGER)
- CAPTAIN AMERICA

Beyond the Director's Cuts, Pyun has also done commentaries on the following physical media releases:

- THE SWORD AND THE SORCERER (BVS): UK, DVD only.
- CYBORG (Shout Factory): North America.
- MEAN GUNS (DigiDreams Studios): Germany, Blu-ray.
- NEMESIS (MVD Entertainment) North America, Blu-ray.
- TICKER (Artisan): North America, DVD only.
- URBAN MENACE (Sterling) North America, DVD only.
- THE WRECKING CREW (Sterling) North America, DVD only.

THE RESPECTABLE PERIOD

NEMESIS 3 (1996) - POSTMORTEM (1998)

A period defined by medium sized Pyun films that were solid, didn't rock the boat, and paid the bills. It includes Pyun's last theatrical released (ADRENALIN: FEAR THE RUSH), some straight genre efforts (BLAST) and a few gems (MEAN GUNS).

NEMESIS 3: TIME LAPSE (1996)

CAST
Sue Price, Tim Thomerson, Norbert Weisser

WRITER
Albert Pyun

PRODUCERS
Tom Karnowski, Gary Schmoeller

CINEMATOGRAPHER
George Mooradian

MUSIC
Anthony Riparetti

PRODUCTION DESIGNERS
Rob Bowen,
Tracy Hennigan

EDITOR
Ken Morrisey

COSTUME DESIGN
Shelly Boies

RUNTIME
85 mins

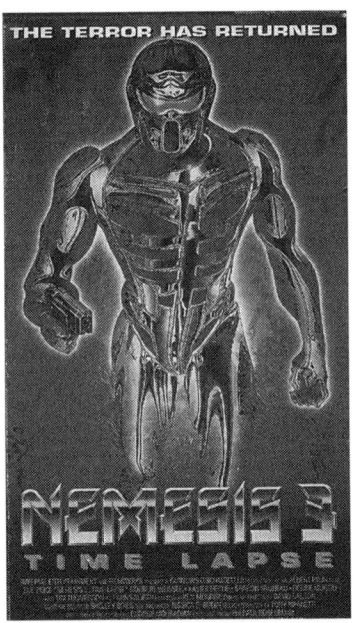

BACK OF THE BOX In this wasteland of despair the path to redemption is not clear. But Alex - a mutant created with super human DNA - carries the seed of hope for all mankind. In a struggle for domination that will never end the Cyborg enemy - designed by humans as a weapon without a soul - will not stop until spark of humanity is eliminated. The Cyborgs are back, here and now, and stronger than ever. The horror has returned we must face what they bring.

WAITING FOR NEMESIS, BY SAMUEL BECKETT

Albert Pyun was given money to make NEMESIS 2 and 3. He spent all the money on PART 2, so instead of throwing in the towel (which most sane people would do), he went ahead and made PART 3 with absolutely no resources. I can confidently say the final result has human beings photographed on film. And they're mostly in focus. That's something to be proud of!

The plot begins with Sue Price (the star of previous entry) waking up with amnesia in the desert. After a long opening credit sequence, we are treated to an endless stretch of clips of the prior NEMESIS, and then we hang out with Tim Thomerson near a jeep, and then we get more flashbacks, and then everyone hangs out in a warehouse.

The plot has something to do with repopulating the earth with muscular women. Did I mention the flashbacks never stop? There's no action. No excitement. The story has the gall to finish up by looping back to the beginning. We are all trapped in video purgatory. Pyun tries to spice things up by filling the frame with women

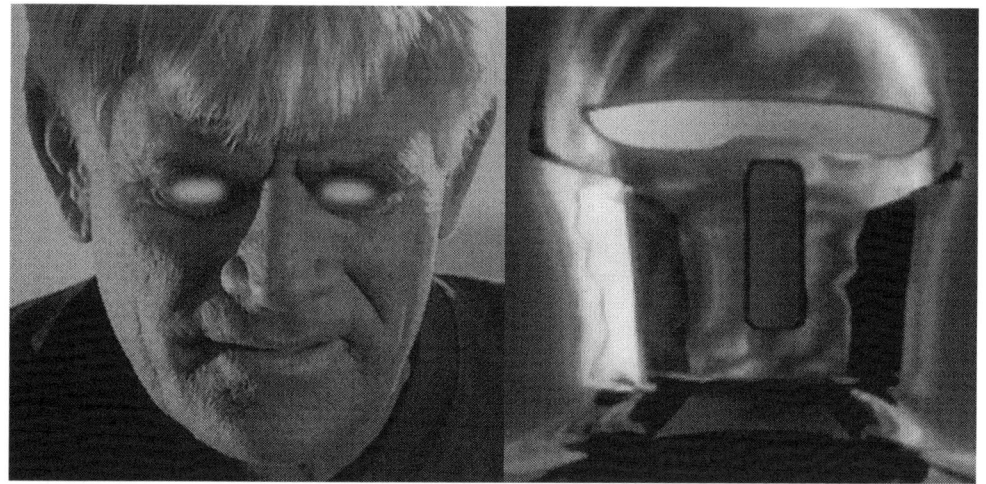

bodybuilders, but other than being a novelty in an action film (again), they don't have anything to do.

NEMESIS 3: TIME LAPSE is not a movie. It's a way to fill up the tape. I'd be curious to know how long Pyun's version would be if he hadn't been forced to stretch it out to an interminable 85 minutes, but then there would need to be something enjoyable to keep. It's a movie that exists only to anger anyone gullible enough to go, "Hey! I liked the first NEMESIS. I didn't know they made a sequel! Let's watch the third one."

This movie signalled the arrival of a tool that would come to redefine Pyun's visual style: Computer Generated Imagery. Tim Thomerson has hilarious green glowing eyes. Sue Price is shocked by cartoon bolts of electricity. The cars in the film are covered over by big digital blobs. I'll be the first to jump to Pyun's defence over most things, but I draw the line when it comes to his use of CGI, which is often random and intrusive. It would be one thing if he used to give things a surreal, otherworldly feel, but it just seems like the CGI in NEMESIS 3 was dropped in without much thought. If anything, I'm glad that a shirtless Tim Thomerson got a paycheque, because I did laugh when Pyun turned him into a crummy looking CGI cyborg.

ADRENALIN: FEAR THE RUSH (1996)

CAST
Christopher Lambert, Natasha Henstridge, Norbert Weisser

WRITER
Albert Pyun

PRODUCERS
Tom Karnowski, Gary Schmoeller

CINEMATOGRAPHER
George Mooradian

MUSIC
Anthony Riparetti

PRODUCTION DESIGNER
Nenad Pecur

EDITOR
Ken Morrisey

COSTUME DESIGN
Shelly Boies

RUNTIME
87 mins

BACK OF THE BOX This pulse-pounding adventure stars dynamic screen hero Christopher Lambert (Highlander I, II and III) as a hard edge police officer locked in a desperate do-or-die race against time. Teamed with a rookie cop (Natasha Henstridge, TV's Eli Stone) he must quickly track down a savage murderer who threatens the world with his contagious disease. But when the chase leads inside the killer's dungeon, the hunters find that they have become the hunted.

NO ONE LIKES ADRENALIN: FEAR THE RUSH.

The plot follows a police team in a ruined future, led by Natasha Henstridge and Christopher Lambert, as they chase an infected monster man through a crumbling Romanian prison.

Lambert and Henstridge are engaging B-movie presences, but all they get to do in ADRENALIN is scream and wheeze through a running time that refuses to give them any way connect with an audience. It isn't difficult to see why Miramax (booooo!) demanded Pyun do re-shoots to spice up the action. Pyun did what was asked of him, and Bob Weinstein still took it out of his hands, added a blue tint, redid the sound mix, and cut it down from 110 to 76 minutes. Miramax dumped the film in theatres, and it was roundly criticized as being devoid of any character, action, or humour — all true, I might add — before being forgotten.

Of course, I find it fascinating.

If you've been reading this book from the start, you know I don't give a free pass to every Albert Pyun film. I find some of his projects just plain uninspired, no matter how heroically he was able to overcome all the obstacles in his path to deliver a final product. It's impressive that Pyun was able to make BLOODMATCH in a few days on the sets of KICKBOXER 2, but that does not make BLOODMATCH enjoyable. The best Pyun films are the ones where he goes in with a high concept goal in mind. It's why something like RADIOACTIVE DREAMS is way more interesting to me than a studio gig like CAPTAIN AMERICA.

I was unsurprised to learn that ADRENALIN was one of Pyun's mad high-concept gambles: he wanted to shoot a film that took place in real-time: A incident happens, a group goes to investigate, and we follow their descent into hell. Everything superfluous in ADRENALIN has been stripped away. There's no joy, limited characterization, and everything is ugly as sin. ADRENALIN was the first project Pyun shot in Slovakia, and he takes great pleasure in displaying the country's rotting buildings on screen. As the police team crawl deeper into the building's black heart, every mouldy wet frame feels like it's caked in cancer. It's even scarier when you consider that none of it was arranged. It just looked like that when they arrived on location.

The star baggage Lambert (HIGHLANDER) and Henstridge (SPECIES) bring to the picture serves as a false promise. The viewer keeps expecting them both to perform big, heroic things, but they never do, so the audience finds themselves trapped, waiting for any kind of release. It's the closest cinema has ever come to replicating the feeling of playing a game like RESIDENT EVIL: You wander around a building, almost in a daze, and wait for something to jump out at you. Where most movies would inject a bunch of new elements to spice up a narrative adaptation, Pyun simply follows a handful of bodies walk through a rotting environment until they die screaming. The "wandering video game" aesthetic is something that director Christophe Gans would attempt to replicate in his adaptation of SILENT HILL (2006), but he failed because he over-explained things. Pyun doesn't make that mistake. For one of the few times in his career, he just lets things be.

If you've read this far, you must be thinking, "Well, that doesn't sound like a very pleasurable experience," and I don't blame you. My enjoyment of the film is principally a reaction to its unique purity. It should be noted that I was able to watch the 102-minute European cut of the film, which still incorporates all the re-shoots, but is much closer to Pyun's original vision. The studio-mandated 76-minute version eliminates any tension or mood and the meddling results in a final product that compresses everything into a shapeless mass.

FUN FACT
Miramax may have released ADRENALIN theatrically, but it was still a quickie job by Pyun. He shot the film in 16 days and only had Christopher Lambert for ten of those.

NEMESIS 4: DEATH ANGEL (1996)

CAST
Sue Price, Blanka Copikova, Andrew Divoff

WRITER
Albert Pyun

PRODUCERS
Tom Karnowski, Gary Schmoeller

CINEMATOGRAPHER
George Mooradian

MUSIC
Anthony Riparetti

PRODUCTION DESIGNER
Nenad Pecur

EDITOR
Ken Morrisey

COSTUME DESIGN
Elizabeth Jett

RUNTIME
80 mins

BACK OF THE BOX Six years after the Cyborg War, an incredibly muscular woman assassin armed with DNA-enhanced fighting skills kills the wrong victim, sparking a deadly battle of redemption.

"SAY TEN HAIL MARYS AND GO TO CYBORG HELL"
— ALEX SINCLAIR (SUE PRICE) BEFORE SHE BLOWS A PRIEST AWAY.

NEMESIS 4: DEATH ANGEL (or CRY OF ANGELS if you go by the credits) was the last "Fuck you" film Pyun made on a studio's dime. It came into existence because Bob Weinstein forced Pyun to head back to Bratislava, Slovakia to do re-shoots on ADRENALIN: FEAR THE RUSH.

Never one to let a chance to make a film go to waste, Pyun decided to make an entirely new feature as he had done with DECEIT and BLOODMATCH. DEATH ANGEL may say its a sequel to NEMESIS on the box, but the only links are the appearance of cyborgs and the return of Sue Price (sporting a radically different look) as the lead.

This time around, Alex Sinclair (Sue Price) is a cyborg assassin who botches a job and goes on the run. She walks through the ruins of Bratislava, has sex in cars, and is followed by a mysterious Woman in Black (Blanka Copikova). Don't get too excited. Like its contractually mandated predecessor NEMESIS 3: TIME-LAPSE, this film is not an action picture by any stretch of the imagination. There's some weird make-up jobs, a handful of nifty-looking guns, and Bratislava makes for an impressive background (as per usual), but PART 4 has the same anemic pace and lack of set-pieces of Albert's previous 3-to-5-day wonders.

Pyun has said in interviews that he wanted to make the film as "Cyberpunk" as possible, but I'm not sure we both interpret that word in the same way. If NEMESIS 4 is any indication, Pyun believes it means slathering on tons of weird softcore sex. Yep, that means Sue Price goes full frontal and participates in many erotic scenes, mostly in cramped European cars. There's so much naked coupling that the film could rest comfortably behind the beaded curtains of your local video store.

Pyun has had no qualms in admitting that the film was an opportunity for him to highlight his love for female bodybuilders. The only real sour note for like-minded aficionados may be that every sex scene climaxes with a gross Cronenberg inspired gore gag — like when a needle pops out of Sue Price's breast, and she impales it through a man's head. The cheap crumbling vibe and the minimal goofy gore effects reminded me at times of the (terrible) output of NYC trash maker Tim Kincaid (MUTANT HUNT), but there's a little more artistry with Pyun at the helm.

If I wanted to be particularly generous, I would say this is kind of like Pyun's take on Godard's ALPHAVILLE (1965) — an experimental piece masquerading as a genre outing. In an interview with Pyun in David J. Moore's great book WORLDS GONE WILD, the writer/director backs up my hypothesis: "It was really the result of my angst over what was happening to ADRENALIN, and I think that influenced some of the philosophical speeches in NEMESIS 4 where I was questioning my own selling out and my own soul searching for who I was as a filmmaker."

OMEGA DOOM (1996)

CAST
Rutger Hauer, Shannon Whirry, Norbert Weisser

WRITERS
Ed Naha, Albert Pyun

PRODUCERS
Tom Karnowski, Gary Schmoeller

CINEMATOGRAPHER
George Mooradian

MUSIC
Anthony Riparetti

PRODUCTION DESIGNER
Nenad Pecur

EDITORS
Ken Morrisey, Joe Shugart

COSTUME DESIGN
Shelly Boies

RUNTIME
84 mins

BACK OF THE BOX In the post-apocalyptic world that is earth, machines rule. Having killed off their human adversaries, the Roms and the Droids have squared off against one another in the search of mankind's last and most fatal weapon of war: Guns. When Omega Doom (Rutger Hauser) strides into the fray, the machines hone in on the stranger and the slaughter intensifies. As combatant's are decimated and the survivors get close to the mystical stash of the guys, the question becomes "Will there be anything left to kill?"

A MINIMALIST RIFF on Dashiell Hammett's RED HARVEST (or YOJIMBO/A FISTFUL OF DOLLARS), Pyun's interpretation of the material is set in the picturesque ruins of an abandoned apartment square in Bratislava, Slovakia. OMEGA DOOM stars a deadpan Rutger Hauer as a Soldier Bot who wanders into a small enclave and finds two groups of robots, the slow Droids and the lethal Roms have reached a stalemate. They've both stood vigil over the same place for years, a mere dozen feet from each other, because they believe there's a secret cache of guns hidden nearby. They fear the humans will return, and the weapons may be their only line of defence.

It should be noted that every character in the film moves at half speed, as if they were all in desperate need of a little oil, and are accompanied by never-ending creaking sound effects. Rutger Hauer slowly, ever so slowly, pits both groups against each other in philosophical (and physical) combat. It's the kind of story where nothing much happens, but every conversation is dripping with existential angst. Oh, and there's a Teacher Droid (Norbert Weisser) who can't keep his damn head on his shoulders.

One of the more hollow catchphrases in film criticism is the classic, "If this were made in the _____ by _____, people would like it more!"

Variations include:

"If this were made in the '80s with practical effects…"

"If this were made in black and white in the '40s…"

"If this were part of the French New Wave…"

And the one that went through my mind throughout the entirety of OMEGA DOOM:

"If this were in another language and sold as an art film, people would like it more…"

I don't think Omega Doom would be considered a classic — it's too minor for that — but I think people would be so much kinder to Pyun's output if his films were draped in more intellectually-appealing clothes. Maybe if they were in any other language than English and came from a different country? Robert Rodriguez said that audiences thought his debut EL MARIACHI was much more profound because it was shot in Spanish and had subtitles.

Pyun has said his main inspirations were European art films by auteurs like Jean-Luc Godard and Ingmar Bergman. By consequence, he always tried to make his projects more profound than people expected, even if was sometimes to the detriment of a film's straight-forward entertainment value. The people that picked OMEGA DOOM off the video wanted a breezy action-packed sci-fi ride where Rutger Hauer blows away robots and drops funny quips . The didn't want a difficult meditation on the nature of existence.

Pyun spent his career trapped in a no man's land between genre and experimentation. He made films that disappointed seven-day renters and wouldn't be touched with a ten foot pole by the art-house crowd. His only way out was to keep making movies and hope someone would notice his hard work and give him a chance to do something different.

It never happened.

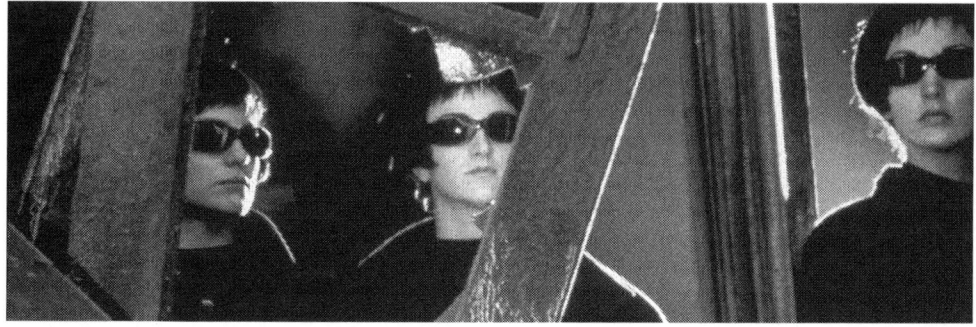

RAVEN HAWK (1996)

CAST
Rachel McLish, John Enos III, Ed Lauter

WRITER
Kevin Alyn Elders

PRODUCER
Ron Samuels

CINEMATOGRAPHER
George Mooradian

MUSIC
Johnny Harris

PRODUCTION DESIGNER
E. Colleen Saro

EDITOR
Dennis M. O'Connor

COSTUME DESIGN
Shelly Busalacchi

RUNTIME
88 mins

BACK OF THE BOX Two-time Ms. Olympia and four-time world champion bodybuilder Rachel McLish is Raven Hawk, a modern day Shoshone Indian wrongly accused of murdering her parents and sentenced to a maximum security asylum,. Twelve years later, she escapes from prison and confronts the villains who killed her parents who are slowly destroying her fellow Shoshone people with the construction of a nuclear waste facility on tribal land. McLish does her own stunts in this intense action drama.

"THE MEDIUM IS THE MESSAGE... WHEN YOU'RE WATCHING A TV MOVIE DIRECTED BY ALBERT PYUN."
— Something no one has ever said, but me

I'VE HEARD people compare RAVEN HAWK to Steven Seagal's bananas film ON DEADLY GROUND (1994), but it's closer to something like Sergio Corbucci's spaghetti revenge western NAVAJO JOE (1966). Burt Reynolds starred in NAVAJO in brown-face, and while it doesn't get that bad in RAVEN HAWK, it should be noted that McLish is not Native American. She does a solid job as a mostly mute avenger, who methodically kills the men on her list, and acrobatically dodges every attack thrown her way. She faces off against a murderer's row of B-villains that include Ed Lauter, Mitch Pileggi, John De Lancie, and regular Pyun Players Thom Mathews and Vincent Klyn. The film keeps the short action bits coming, but it fumbles the payoffs due to a lack of gore, which is odd because it was produced and aired on HBO.

I'm not going to go out on a limb and say this is some lost classic, but it does look (if I squint) like a solid western action film that would be helped immensely by a new video transfer. Albert Pyun obsessed over the visual textures of his movies. He and cinematographer George Mooradian would pick a specific stock to create the story's intended mood. They would use a ridiculous number of filters to achieve a unique look and seriously considered what brand of light would give them the proper emotional effect for a scene. I asked George if he modified his approach knowing the films would go straight to video (Or TV in this case) and he said, "I put that aside. Everything to me was going to be a major motion picture."

Albert and George worked during a time where theatrical films and straight-to-video productions all used the same equipment. George even insisted that all of his movies be shot anamorphically — even if no audience was ever going to be able to appreciate his hard work because the major release format was full-screen video. Even when DVD arrived, Pyun's films were often released in pan-and-scan transfers. Why would a distributor  put in the work to make KICKBOXER 2: THE WAY BACK look as good as it could if they thought the consumer couldn't tell the difference? The films were given the treatment the companies thought they deserved as disposable genre entertainment: the bare minimum.

It wasn't until the advent of Blu-ray and streaming that things changed. You can watch a beautiful looking widescreen print of BRAINSMASHER...A LOVE STORY on Amazon Prime that captures the gorgeous details of the Mooradian's nighttime photography. Thanks to Blu-ray distributors like MVD, even a lesser film like CRAZY SIX can be appreciated in all of its candy coloured glory. Does it make the movie more cohesive? Nope! But it does reveal a whole other layer of artistry to appreciate.

This is a long way for me to go to say that it's a challenge for me to review RAVEN HAWK properly. The only copy I could find was pan and scan. For some movies, you can watch a motion stabilized version on YouTube and still get the full impact, but that's not the case here. For one, it's a straight-ahead homage to the Spaghetti Westerns of the late '60s, so it needs to feel big. The deserts, the horses, and the figures should appear a hundred feet tall in front of George Mooradian's lens — and it looks like he shot it that way! RAVEN HAWK appeared on Laserdisc with a 2.35:1 widescreen transfer, but I wasn't able to find it anywhere at a reasonable price, and even then it wouldn't hold a candle to a good Blu-ray.

MEAN GUNS (1997)

CAST
Christopher Lambert, Ice-T, Michael Halsey

WRITER
Andrew Witham

PRODUCERS
Tom Karnowski, Gary Schmoeller

CINEMATOGRAPHER
George Mooradian

MUSIC
Anthony Riparetti

PRODUCTION DESIGNER
(Uncredited)

EDITOR
Ken Morrisey

COSTUME DESIGN
Shelly Boies

RUNTIME
84 mins

BACK OF THE BOX The world's most dangerous criminals are summoned to a new prison on the eve before its grand opening by Moon (Ice T), the ruthless leader of the world's most powerful crime syndicate. Chaos ensues when weapons and ammunition are passed around the group, including Lou (Christopher Lambert), begin their fight to survive. The last three men standing by midnight have been promised $10,000,000 in cash by Moon, who watches from his surveillance camera as gunfire and bodies fly. Rivalries develop between friends and the liens of loyalty are crossed as each criminal attempt to outwit, outrun and outlive the other in this action packed game of elimination.

THE FIRST ALBERT PYUN FILM

I fell in love with was MEAN GUNS. I must have read about it on the Kung Fu Cult Cinema forum back in the day, or maybe I was in a Christopher Lambert kind of mood at the time, but something pushed me to grab it as part of an HMV two-DVDs-for-$14 deal. Maybe I just liked that the word GUNS was in the title? I was an easy mark. I paired it with U.S. SEALS II directed by Isaac Florentine (another soon to be favourite director) and never looked back.

I'm a little surprised that I was so open to MEAN GUNS at the time. I was a picky film goer who unfairly demanded that all action scenes have the grandeur and acrobatic choreography of John Woo. MEAN GUNS doesn't even have any squibs! It did have a Hong Kong feel to it, but it also took place in one location, had a pitifully low budget, and the pan-n-scan DVD transfer was atrocious on the eyes.

It didn't matter. I was smitten. I loved the fact that it was one long gunfight, sported a distinct look, and had the guts to commit to an all-mambo soundtrack (by Tony Riparetti of course). I didn't care that the script was a bastard child of the post-Tarantino era. I was won over by the fact that it's evident everyone wanted to make the most entertaining film they could. It felt like the work of a passionate director with vision. Plus, it had a body count that numbered in the hundreds.

MEAN GUNS is one of those rare times that everything worked for Pyun (see also: NEMESIS). He got to shoot it in LA, had a great location at his disposal (a soon to be opened prison) and his ace DP George Mooradian figured out a simple, but striking, way to quickly light the location.

Ice-T growls through his role as the main villain. Christopher Lambert yucks it up as a blond-dyed assassin, and while he shot his role in only two and a half days (and was paid two million for it), you'd never know. The rest of the cast is made up of old and new Pyun Players: Thom Mathews, Yuji Okumoto, Michael Halsey and Tina Cote all get to chew up the scenery as flamboyant criminals.

The main issue during the shoot was that the production had to make sure not to damage the location (which was going to open soon), which meant squibs and pyrotechnics were out of the question. It's odd at first to see so many people fire guns that cause no visible damage, but once you get over the compromise, it stops being an issue. The stylized lighting scheme helps. The sterile prison set is often illuminated in large patches of blown-out white light that seem to indicate the story is taking place somewhere between earth and heaven.

MEAN GUNS is a great starter film for people new to the work of Albert Pyun. It doesn't have the polish of his earlier pictures like NEMESIS, but it does feature low-budget ingenuity by the ton and should quickly get curious viewers hooked on the Pyun bandwagon.

Just make sure to watch the remastered widescreen version!

FUN FACT

I recently watched MEAN GUNS and realized that Albert Pyun was doing a riff on Johnnie To's Hong Kong classic THE MISSION (1999). Pyun uses the same stripped-down, wide-angle, hiding-behind-pillars action aesthetic featured in To's film, but Albert stretches it out to 90 minutes. To my surprise, I discovered THE MISSION came out two years later. Pyun was once again ahead of the game.

BLAST (1997)

CAST
Linden Ashby, Andrew Divoff, Kimberly Warren

WRITER
Albert Pyun (as Hannah Blue)

PRODUCERS
Tom Karnowski, Gary Schmoeller

CINEMATOGRAPHER
George Mooradian

MUSIC
Anthony Riparetti

PRODUCTION DESIGNER
Shelly Boies

EDITOR
Natasha Gjurokovic

COSTUME DESIGN
Shelly Boies

RUNTIME
105 mins

BACK OF THE BOX The world's finest athletes have once again gathered for a sports competition. Security is airtight as world leaders set aside global conflicts in order to celebrate the purity of sports. Just before the competition begins, a deadly team of terrorists mount a precision attack on the swimming complex, holds the Women's swimming team hostage and unknowingly traps a janitor (Linden Ashby) within the sprawling compound. The terrorists wire each competition venue with a deadly fission explosive and then uplink to a global satellite to announce their plans to a stunned international audience. For emphasis, the head terrorist murders a swimmer as billions of horrified viewers watch in helpless silence. Totally unprepared for an assault of this magnitude, a desperate President and the F.B.I enlists the brilliant Interpol counter-terrorist expert LEO (Rutger Hauer) who coordinates his efforts with the trapped janitor to contain the volatile situation.

BLAST is a DIE HARD clone shorn to its base elements: one location, a single protagonist, and a group of terrorists that need to be defeated. Nothing more, nothing less. In this case, the blue-collar hero (Linden Ashby) was once a taekwondo champion, but some bad life choices have led him to work at an Olympic pool as a janitor with a limp. On the day his ex-wife (Kimberly Warren) visits the pool with her swim team, the building is taken over by a group of terrorists (led by Pyun Player Andrew Divoff), and it's up to our hero to take them all down.

It's boilerplate stuff, but Pyun's method is to approach it all from the most minimalistic of angles. There are no jokes, funny one-liners, or wacky set-pieces. It's so lean at times that it plays like a heist sequence from a Jean-Pierre Melville film (LE CERCLE ROUGE, LE SAMOURAI): quiet, exact, and professional. The story even drops the protagonist after a brief introduction and focuses on Divoff and his gang as they execute their plan in rigorous detail.

When Linden Ashby finally realizes something is going on (40 minutes in), he spends the next 30 minutes completely silent (beyond a single "shit") as he tries to stop the baddies. Fights are had. Bullets are fired. The hero is repeatedly injured.

The structure is simple in a way that is rare in Pyun's oeuvre, and it's nice to see him pull it off so effectively. I've seen a lot of people call BLAST generic, but I still find its no-frills execution impressive. It's not lazy, just focused. It has razor-sharp cinematography by George Mooradian, a meaty score by Tony Riparetti, and a cast peppered with Pyun's regulars: Thom Mathews shows up as the film's Harry Ellis-like weasel and Tim Thomerson plays a government official. The only off-key element is the presence of Rutger Hauer as a wheelchair-bound terrorist expert, made up in brown face and clothed in Native American attire. The tastelessness is never commented on, so I assume it's something Hauer wanted to do.

BLAST is excellent proof that Pyun could deliver straightforward cinematic thrills without stepping out of bounds.

RECOMMENDATIONS

I love the simplicity of the DIE HARD template and some of my favourites include:

NO CONTEST (1995): Shannon Tweed is in a beauty pageant when terrorist Andrew Dice Clay and Rowdy Roddy Piper take over the building. Directed by Paul Lynch (PROM NIGHT).

RED WOLF (1995): On New Year's Eve, a boat is taken over by terrorists and its left up to super kicker Kenny Ho to save the day. Directed by Yuen Woo-Ping, one of the best action choreographers ever.

AUTOMATIC (1995): While working late one night, a woman witnesses a murder, and it's up to a cyborg security guard (Olivier Gruner) to get her out of the building. It's a rare "perfect storm" movie where all the elements come together, but the creative team never did anything else of note.

CRAZY SIX (1997)

CAST
Rob Lowe, Burt Reynolds, Mario Van Peebles

WRITER
Galen Yuen

PRODUCERS
Tom Karnowski, Gary Schmoeller

CINEMATOGRAPHER
George Mooradian

MUSIC
Anthony Riparetti

PRODUCTION DESIGNER
Nenad Pecur

EDITOR
Natasha Gjurokovic

COSTUME DESIGN
Gini Kramer

RUNTIME
94 mins

BACK OF THE BOX The eastern block has fallen and Communism is dead. In its place has come new opportunity - but not without a deadly price. Powerful Mafia families have emerged from the anarchy to vie for control of the lucrative underground weapons and technology trade. Crazy Six (Rob Lowe, THE WEST WING) and Dirty Mao (Mario Van Peebles, NEW JACK CITY) are the leaders of two rivalling mob families, who agree to form an uneasy alliance in order to overthrow Raul (Ice T, NEW JACK CITY), the leader of one of the largest crime cartels in Europe. But when the mission goes awry, the place turns into a deadly battleground with three world class gangsters fight each other to the death.

"COMMUNISM IS DEAD. OPPORTUNITY IS IN."
— THE FILM'S TAGLINE

At a certain point, Albert Pyun's films all started to take place in purgatory.

Every location is cramped. The visuals are claustrophobic. All the characters are trapped in an impossible situation with no chance of salvation. It's the premise of URBAN MENACE, NEMESIS 3: TIME LAPSE, and OMEGA DOOM. This is obviously the result of budget limitations, but it's also a state of mind. The walls were closing in on Pyun's film making career, and with no opportunity to escape, he could only paint his frustrations out on the screen. CRAZY SIX is the slickest version of that prison.

We follow a grizzled Rob Lowe, the titular Crazy Six, as he slums around the streets of Bratislava, Slovakia after a heist. Sadly, there aren't six crazy guys. It's just a nickname Lowe's character got because he was the sixth child in his family. And he's crazy! (Not really). Burt Reynolds (in a cowboy hat) is the cop hot on Six's trail. Ivana Milicevic (who spends most of the film singing) plays a hooker with a heart of gold. Ice-T (who rarely

gets out of his chair) is a mob boss out for revenge. Mario Van Peebles (with a French accent) pets a tiny dog.

We've been to all these Slovakian locations before in Pyun's filmography, so cinematographer George Mooradian decides to bathe everything in hallucinogenic primary coloured light. Tony Riparetti's score never lets up. The viewer gets an early taste of Pyun's hyper-stylized editing patterns (why cut when you can fade?) that would soon become the norm. The script by Galen Yuen has zero drive, but it's static nature paired with Pyun's stylistic overdrive results in the project having a surreal David Lynchian vibe by way of Abel Ferrara: Weirdo criminals trapped in a rainbow dimension without a chance of salvation in sight.

The meandering narrative would soon become the norm in Pyun's filmography, but this is undoubtedly his most polished illustration of waiting around for nothing to happen. Even the opening contextual titles pop in blazing neon colours. It is at once Pyun at his most desperate (there's no story) and most artful (why not experiment a little?) with a budget that allows him to indulge in his vices without fraying at the seams (as long as you don't expect any action). It's an oppressive freak-out destined to disappoint people unfamiliar with Pyun's latter day style.

Thankfully, I can soak up the flights of folly in CRAZY SIX because I know it's Albert's penultimate trip before his banishment to the digital wastelands. That's when the real hard times start.

And there really is no escape.

FUN FACT The film was initially meant to be shot in San Francisco, which would have robbed it of its crumbling mood, but may have tied it even closer to the sun-baked creepiness of David Lynch's oeuvre.

POSTMORTEM
(1998)

CAST
Charlie Sheen, Michael Halsey, Ivana Milicevic

WRITERS
John Lowry Lamb, Robert McDonnell

PRODUCERS
Tom Karnowski, Gary Schmoeller

CINEMATOGRAPHER	**MUSIC**	**PRODUCTION DESIGNER**
George Mooradian	Anthony Riparetti	Pat Campbell
EDITOR	**COSTUME DESIGN**	**RUNTIME**
Natasha Gjurokovic	Lynn Aitken	105 mins

BACK OF THE BOX James McGregor (Sheen), a serial killer profiler turned novelist, flees to a small, peaceful town to escape his violent past. But the peace and tranquillity are only temporary as the town is stalked by a cold-blooded killer who creates obituaries of his victims before he kills them: forcing McGregor back into the life he longs to leave behind...

POSTMORTEM is the end of an era for Albert Pyun. The wide angles and coloured lighting are present, but they're utilized in a much more restrained fashion. There are no quick cuts, scenes are mostly captured in one lengthy steadicam shot, and the entire production has time to breathe in a way Pyun's films rarely do. Of course, you could argue that this calmer style is the result of another impossible ten-day schedule, but then you'd have to ignore how thoughtfully put together it all is. You'd never know that Charlie Sheen was only available for six days of the ten-day shoot. He's affable in the lead, but there's not much for him to do, and while the story does spend a generous amount of time following the killer, the script does little to invoke

the viewer's sympathy. It's a relatively straight-faced affair with very suspense or gore (but there is an abundant amount of clinical nudity.) The film is not bad, just a little too anonymous in its content. It's simply another serial killer procedural in the mould of SILENCE OF THE LAMBS/KISS THE GIRLS/THE BONE COLLECTOR. POSTMORTEM plays like a TV movie at times, but a few stand-out moments — like a chase through the streets of Glasgow and a showdown at a picturesque cemetery — hint at a different side of Pyun he never had a chance to revisit. It made me wonder if there was an alternate career path he could have followed in the mannered style of POSTMORTEM, instead of the desperate form his cinema would take.

Probably not.

Pyun's gotta Pyun.

POSTMORTEM was the last film George Mooradian shot for Albert. They had worked together since KICKBOXER 2 (1991) and would not collaborate again.

I asked George if he felt things were coming to an end during the production.

He said he didn't.

They just drifted apart.

FUN FACT The film was initially supposed to be set in San Francisco (like CRAZY SIX and TICKER) but moved to Glasgow, so Tony Riparetti goes all in with a fun Scottish-flavoured score, which was the first (and last) time he got to use an orchestra for an Albert Pyun picture.

INTERVIEW
GEORGE MOORADIAN
(CINEMATOGRAPHER)

Were you always interested in working in the film industry?

Well, it wasn't Hollywood movies that got me interested, but esoteric documentaries and the interesting rhythms of Eastern European films. In college, I didn't know what I wanted to do, so I changed my major to filmmaking, and that was the moment where I decided I wanted to work in this field.

And when did you decide to focus on cinematography?

The Director of Photography job was Mount Olympus, because being a cinematographer back then was something that gods did and there was no way I could get there, but it was okay, I didn't mind doing the slate. I just wanted to be around, do whatever.

You may have started at the bottom, but you worked on a lot of big films! How did you get involved with feature film production?

When I was graduating in Atlanta, I stayed there and worked for free in whatever production that came into town. One summer there was a workshop in Rockport Maine and Vilmos Zsigmond was going to be the guest artist. He flew up right after CLOSE ENCOUNTERS OF THE THIRD KIND from Mobile Alabama. He was somebody that I admired, so I was determined to be a part of the workshop. I drove up in my brother's van, camping out on the way, and spent a week with Vilmos and a small group of people. I was blown away and really connected with him. He said to make a ten-year plan and work towards that. That was easy. In ten years, I hoped to work for Vilmos! That was also the motivating factor to move out to California. Just before I did, he started another movie called THE DEER HUNTER (1978), and I called him from Atlanta, as we had stayed in touch, and he was in Cleveland shooting it, but nobody knew a thing about it. I remember spending $40 on a phone call just talking and trying to work out the logistics on how to get there. I remember him going, "I'm not sure, George. We call this set the Mickey and Bobby Show, Cimino and De Niro, they don't want strangers here." We went back and forth until finally, he got permission, and I joined the camera team. I worked on the wedding sequence, which took about a week to do in the Orthodox Church. I have a picture of me with Vilmos during those days. I was so young and I using the slate in front of Robert De Niro.

After that, I got in my little Toyota and drove cross country and haven't looked back. I wasn't in the Union in California, so I could only work union wise on films in the Midwest. Being in Georgia, I was in the Chicago local, so when Vilmos went to do a John Cassavetes movie FLESH AND BLOOD, I went as his assistant, so that was a big coup for me. He actually moved me out from second assistant to first assistant on the movie THE BORDER (1982) with Jack Nicholson and Harvey Keitel, so somehow, I was on a lot of big movies. My passion came through, I worked hard, I was meticulous, and I really supported the production. In terms of working in LA, some of the first things I got were AFI student films that I worked on for free. I was one of the only ones who knew how a Panaflex worked, so I got my first paying job through that, and it was a $100 for a week with a Russian cinematographer. I worked with Walter Lassally, who won an Oscar for Tom Jones and on, and on. The pinnacle, besides working with Vilmos, was getting to know Vitorrio Storaro. I love THE CONFORMIST, and APOCALYPSE NOW is my favourite, and I was one of the operators on DICK TRACY (1990). I was in heaven.

That must have been a surreal experience.

Every department head was an Academy Award winner. Dick Silver was on the production design. Milena Canonero was on the wardrobe. Of course, there was also Warren Beatty. I got to pick his Italian crew's brain. We had so many conversations. Storaro's first operator, Enrico Umetelli, had done all those incredible camera moves on THE LAST EMPEROR. I didn't want the experience to end!

When did you earn your first credit as a cinematographer?

What happened was, I assisted on a Lech Majewski film called FLIGHT OF THE SPRUCE GOOSE (1986) and Jerzy Zielinski was the DOP. Somehow, I hit it off with Lech while Jerzy was scouting, and he had a scene he wanted to do at the Queen Mary at Long Beach California. I ended up shooting it, and it was his favourite scene in the movie. So he asked me to shoot THE PRISONER OF RIO (1988), and that was my first film as a director of photography.

And how did you get started with Albert?

A friend of mine from Atlanta, Philip Waters, moved out here and connected with Albert through Chuck Minsky (Cinematographer of RADIOACTIVE DREAMS) and Albert had Philip shoot CAPTAIN AMERICA (1990). Since I knew Philip, he asked me to come on as a second DP and operator. We shot in Yugoslavia, and it went super well. The Red Skull's lair was Dubrovnik, the walled city, and we shot up and down the coast. It was still Yugoslavia, but it was in its last days as a country. Our crew was Serbian, Croatian, Bosnian, Slovenian, and you could feel the tension. All our shooting was done in what's now known as Croatia. I was in my element and had a ball. I connected with Albert, and when Philip wasn't available for the next one, he asked me to shoot KICKBOXER 2: THE ROAD BACK (1991).

Did you shoot that film in L.A.?

Yes, L.A. and Irvine. We were at the amphitheatre for UC California. On KICKBOXER 2, I actually wasn't going to be hired. I didn't have enough credits for the money men. So, Albert pulled a ploy and tried to hire Haskell Wexler to appease the executive producers. He told me "George, I know he's going to turn it down," so I got it at the last minute when Haskell said no.

What was your experience like on KICKBOXER 2?

I didn't feel any constrictions! We had a 30 day shooting schedule on that one. Before I met Albert, I was nowhere inclined to do science fiction, or martial arts movies. I'm a serious drama guy, but somehow we had so much fun! We worked with some famous martial artists like Benny The Jet, and Jimmy Nickerson, who choreographed RAGING BULL and some of the ROCKY films, so I grew to know action, how to shoot it, how to do martial arts, and found that it was actually fun. I believe KICKBOXER 2 and NEMESIS were the longest shoots I had with Albert and then it was less, way less. As we got better, they kept reducing the number of days we'd get. If the next one was going to be 24, the one after that was 18, and then 12, and then 8, and finally down to 3 or 4 days...

And how would you describe the collaborative process with Albert?

Well, after we got to know each other, it became less about the physicality and more about discussing the look. Albert was fearless. My job was to always try to scare him. How do I push the limits on the photography? I would always go over and above. You should see some of my scripts. They're covered with notes. A lot of people may not have treated it as seriously as I did, but I dove deep into everything. I wanted to experiment and push the limits.

The movies you worked on with Albert look fantastic.

Thanks for saying that! The L.A. Times, which never mentioned cinematography in their genre reviews, gave me a huge notice for KICKBOXER 2! That felt really, really good. We went to New York because we were so thrilled it was opening theatrically. We even shot some stuff for DOLLMAN and ARCADE at the same time.

Did DOLLMAN (1991) and ARCADE (1991) feel like troubled productions? I've read they were very tough to pull off.

Not that I was aware of. Who was the producer on that? z

Charles Band.

Yeah, the problems were probably with him. We had a ball on those films. Tim Thomerson was great. We really got along. Albert liked familiar faces around. He had his own players, and Tim was always part of it. We filmed DOLLMAN at the same location, Fontana, where they shot TERMINATOR 2, and we did some stuff for NEMESIS there as well. We'd find a location that we liked and multipurpose it. I don't remember anything being troubled. It was like being on a survival march through the Sahara. If you were one or two steps ahead of these Iron Men, and Albert was one of them, that meant you were super efficient. We'd say things like "We're doing this coverage European style," which means you're shooting in one direction and making it look as good as you can with as much production value as possible, with silhouettes, and coverage in profile, but not doing reverses, not doing overs, and all of that worked beautifully.

How difficult was it working with all the visual FX elements on DOLLMAN?

We just jumped in and did them. It was full speed ahead, nothing really daunted us, nothing that I really stumbled on, or couldn't figure out.

Would Albert ever hand you a shot list on set?

We always did whatever was the most visual and worked the best with the actors. We would maximize the location. We did do scouts, which I agreed with because our shooting schedule got so tight, but our crew was very experienced, and to me, that is what made us successful. We all got paid very good rates. We had great steadicam operators. Great gaffers. That was the idea. I did a lot of the prep, so I knew it backwards and forwards. If the first AD was new and wasn't in our groove, they got left by the wayside. We were always moving forward.

That's good to hear! When I read about the productions you worked on with Albert, they sound very stressful, without much money or time.

Maybe I was young and naive, but I was living my dream, and I never found that things were troubled. People would say "George, you love what you're doing!" and I'd be like "Yeah!" because I could make it as artful and dramatic as I wanted. Sometimes, I did have to bring things up, but in general, I was very expressive and very impressionistic, so when I went into television, I had problems with that because the digital realm didn't allow me to express myself like I did with film. I didn't have much of a canvas anymore. Although, my wife says television made me a better cinematographer because it gave me discipline. I had tighter a ratio. The film has a 20 to 1 ratio. When I first started with digital, the ratio was 1:1 or 2:1 and it drove me crazy.

Were there any times when the producers came around and said, Hey! Tone down that crazy artistic style!"?

Yeah, but I was such an integral part of the process, they knew they needed me. I did get some push back on MEAN GUNS because I wanted to cross process some things and shoot it with FUJI stock. They questioned me on that. I was a big believer in testing. I pushed it beyond the limit to show Albert that I had data behind me. Even if it was a three or four day shoot like BLOODMATCH, I would test: "What if I went in this direction? Or overexposed this? And used this filter for nights?" I always had a working idea of where I might be going.

How did you pick the visual look of NEMESIS (1992)?

Basically, we wanted a future that felt lived in, which is why we picked an old sleepy Hawaiian town as opposed to a sleek area. We shot that in SUPER 35 which was spherical, but in a widescreen format that went perf to perf and had a 2.35:1 anamorphic style aspect ratio. After NEMESIS, I got some calls from some big director's about "Ah! How did you do this? Or that?" I got into trouble because if you remember Olivier Gruner runs across that big slag heap near the beginning...

Yeah! There's a very dangerous looking section during the opening gunfight where he's sliding and hiding behind cement blocks.

I had the CHAPMAN TITAN, which was the biggest jib I could get, and on top of that, I put another crane, so I had three or four articulating things that I was operating myself. So to get that working telescoping and moving was a little awkward, but we were able to get in close. And once I sort of worked it out, it was a really dynamic tool to use. Mark Morse was our steadicam operator on those overturned buildings and, he had to be a solid athlete to get through that. I used a lot of strong filtration, the opening is very warm. I used Tobaccos tripled off to get that effect. I think because of the scope, it did turn out bigger and better. MythBusters called me about something on that film.

That's amazing!

Yeah, we were the first to shoot our way out of a gunfight through a floor.

What did MythBusters want to know?

They wanted to know how we did it, and they tried it to see if it could actually be done in real life.

Every time I watch the shot from that sequence of Olivier falling through the floor with the camera pointed up at him I go, "I have no idea how they did that."

I was just going for it. I had harnesses strapped to Olivier's chest with a camera, and that was before Go-Pros, so we had to shoot it with a crane outside looking in.

I have to bring up KNIGHTS (1993) because it's such a beautiful looking movie, especially the way you used filters on the sky...

Did I ever! I used every filter under the sun for that movie, from polarizers to grates, to cranberries, tops, bottoms, left, I literally think I used nine to twelve stage filters on some of those shots. It just lent itself to it. It was in the Mojave desert with Kris Kristofferson. Monument Valley was just dripping with John Ford. It was unbelievable. You can call it a B-Movie, but I was having so much fun. It looks the way it does because we made a pact not to use any artificial lights, and we said we are going to harness the sun. I like hard strong light, and I had mirror board, not reflector boards, doing a lot of the work. There's one sequence where the horses come over the ridge, it's magic hour, and there are shafts of light and dust, and that was all done with some of our picture car headlights! It was that simple.

It really works!

When we first discussed it, I thought the movie should be more earthy, and it was Albert's choice to use more colours. Now, I see where that comes from. I just got back from Morocco, and I realize there were so many bright colours around desert places. A favourite story on KNIGHTS is one night around our campfire, Kris Kristofferson serenaded us with his classic songs. Oh my god, it was so great. The cast loved Albert. Everybody loved Albert. That was a short shooting schedule. It was twelve or eighteen days.

Would Albert share any inspirations before a project started? I feel like KNIGHTS has a real Hong Kong action cinema feel to it.

He was very influenced by that. In fact, on KNIGHTS if we had a stunt that we wanted to follow all the way to the ground, we called it Hong Kong style. He always had the best stunt guys. This was the first film of Chad Stahelski, who would go on to direct the JOHN WICK films. He was a nobody kid at the time, but he was really good with swords and Filipino style fighting. He was brought in by a more seasoned stunt guy, and boy, has Chad taken off. I think he might have been on BRAINSMASHER as well. Another person we discovered from KNIGHTS to BRAINSMASHER was Dave Emmrich, the steadicam operator. KNIGHTS was his first film, and it was heavy steadicam work. We about killed him, but he was young, just out of NYU. He got a lifetime achievement from the Society of Camera Operators.

The style of KNIGHTS, and a lot of the films you worked with Albert on feel about five years ahead of their time. No one in North America was making that kind of action picture.

We didn't quite know! We did two or three movies a year, and that's all we did.

How was your time on BRAINSMASHER... A LOVE STORY?

I always say that movie has one of the best wet down looks ever. It was misting pretty much the whole time in Portland. That was a benefit for me. It was a wacky crazy time. I was on top of a city bus at one point, and you can't do that now. Me and Terri Hatcher teamed up against the stunt guys in a pool match one night and won!

Was Andrew Dice Clay difficult on set? He was coming off quite a career high at that time.

He behaved. Albert was chill and knew how to work with him. I know that Andrew did not like it when I used back-light on him because he had thinning hair. Speaking of hair, I did catch Burt Reynolds hair on fire on CRAZY SIX.

Wow!

His hair, which was artificial, started smoking and he took it really well. He said, "George, it's okay, you can catch me on fire as long as I look good." He was hilarious.

It looks like you shot three films back to back, HONG KONG '97 (1994), SPITFIRE (1995) and HEATSEEKER (1996)...

Yeah! That was some intense cross-blocking and cross-shooting. We did all three films in the Philippines, and it was a trip. I think we did them in four months? SPITFIRE might have been the more commercial one.

It feels like the one with the biggest budget.

We went to Florida to shoot some of the gymnastic stuff at the Olympic training grounds, and then we went to Rome! You know who did our dailies? Technicolor Rome! It's where Vittorio Storaro did his work.

How much of SPITFIRE was filmed without permits? There's a sequence in Hong Kong where it feels like you just went and shot it without shutting down the street.

That was purely guerrilla. We would plan it, drive up, get out of the car, and just shoot it. On HONG KONG '97 we shot on a floating city with Robert Patrick. A 135mm lens on a steadicam with two floating objects, and while it was tough to pull off if Albert thought it was good, it was brilliant.

It sounds like a risky operation.

We spent even less time on HEATSEEKER (1996), which was a big martial arts grand royale.

Did you feel Albert shifting more toward a more long lens style on HEATSEEKER?

Yeah, I would say a lot of that was just to be different than what we were doing before, like KICKBOXER 2 where I was in the ring to make it more visceral, and in HEATSEEKER we wanted to shoot it in a giant Auditorium. We looked at it, scouted it, and I said I'm going to need a week to pre-light it and probably a week or so to shoot and a few days to strike. What happened was, they were having graduations in the auditorium, and it was only going to be available for one or two days. Okay. My solution was to throw manpower at it. My brother was the gaffer, so at 2 AM in the morning, we hired 60 grips and electrics, and they were all lined up like an army. Half of the crew was throwing up from drinking the night before. At 2 AM they let us in the venue, by 8:30 AM we were shooting. It was the biggest crew I ever had, and we just figured it out. I needed to light everything, the ring, the audience, some of the hallways, but that's how I did it. We shot all day, maybe a little the next day, and that was it. We had to get out.

Did the fact that the films were going to be released straight to video affect the way you shot them?

No. I put that aside. I just submerged it. Everything to me was going to be a major motion picture. That's how I approached it. I delude myself all the time. Anything I did with Albert that was straight to video, it turned my stomach. That's why I shot anamorphic and went full blast with what I could do. All the reviews said over and over again, "It doesn't look like a $300,000 movie."

You never went "That's just too ambitious"?

No, it was a good challenge for me. Albert wouldn't hear of any problems. He pushed me. It was my golden age and education. We would shoot way past what any normal person would shoot. It would be pitch black, and we'd be shooting night for day! On NEMESIS, we lost the actor at one point, so we shot in silhouettes so we could hide it. I never said no. We shot pieces of the same scene in two different states.

Where you and Albert aware of the critical reactions to your films?

I was, and it did get to me, especially near the end. At some point, I hoped we would break through to do more commercial and mainstream work, but it just wasn't in Albert's soul. The couple of times we did get a little bigger, like for Miramax on ADRENALIN, they screwed it all up.

The studio put a tint on your footage!

Albert didn't have a great time on that. It was more Bob than Harvey. It was as close as we got to breaking through.

I love the original look of the film. It's very wet and mouldy.

That was our first film in Bratislava. We liked that better than Prague because it was an unrestored old town. Prague was more like Disneyland. If you see that, OMEGA DOOM, one of the NEMESIS movies, and CRAZY SIX, all of those films have so much texture and we could still walk to work. You remember the opening riots in ADRENALIN?

Oh yeah.

I did all that operating with knee pads on. Very visceral.

Was ADRENALIN shot in twelve days?

It was very short! We were successful, though. Albert didn't dictate much. I do remember in one movie, Albert wanted the tone of SILENCE OF THE LAMBS.

POSTMORTEM?

Yeah! He didn't want to overemphasize the horror.

What were the crews like in Bratislava?

How that progressed was that on our first movie there (ADRENALIN), I brought in a lot of my crew. My brother as the gaffer, and other people as key grip, first, second and steadicam operator. I think by the second film it was just me. My crew was Slovakian, and my keys were Croatian. I made it work! I pride myself in being able to communicate with only a few phrases and words. And as opposed to here, my photography there was less grip intensive. The grips there mostly just move the camera. They don't set up the lights, do flagging, or rigging. If you get a light, a big light, in the right position, it does all the work. That's why I was using big directional jumbo lights. It just kind of worked that way for our European style of coverage. I was able to move along efficiently. I operated the camera, and my favourite was the Australian Moviecam. Usually, I'd use the ARRI BL. Not so much the Panaflex. The BL would be too heavy for steadicam and for hand holding. The Moviecam was modular.

Would you shoot with multiple cameras?

Not very often. We did for some of the stunts, but a lot of the shots were choreographed with a dolly or steadicam with one camera, like MEAN GUNS (1997). That's one of my favourites.

Me too!

It's still on my reel! We shot that in the City Central jail, a billion dollar complex before it opened. Albert said, "Let's make a movie!" It was me on a pee-wee dolly as we rolled around and got all those shots. Way over exposed. It's got a great feel to it. And the soundtrack, the mambo, I love it. The shell casings falling. All the speed ups and slow downs.

How was shooting CRAZY SIX (1997)?

I would say it was one of the less connected ones. But we had Burt Reynolds, Mario Van Peebles, Rob Lowe, and that made it fun for me! And it got me Mario Van Peebles next movie LOVE KILLS (1998). Again, I was trying to make it as interesting, weird and colourful as I could. Since we'd been there so many times, I just tried to do something different again.

And after that, there was OMEGA DOOM (1996)...

That was a location that was supposed to be in Anaheim, and be a Disneyland-esque dystopia. It was so strange. In my ASC profile, they asked what was one of the most satisfying things I ever did, and I said OMEGA DOOM. It's when I had a scene where I was operating with Rutger Hauer, and I created light and shadow for him to play with. It was one of the more memorable moments I've ever had. Again, it was very strange. How can you go to mainstream work after all that?

You worked with Rutger on BLAST (1997) as well.

On BLAST, we had Rutger Hauer for a single day. That was a short schedule.

Do you have any memories of Tom Karnowski? He was with Albert for so long as a producer, but I can barely find any information on him.

They grew up together in Hawaii. They were childhood friends. He was the one I dealt with for all the financials and logistics. He was a decent, honourable guy who made deals with my crew. Very savvy. He was also a camera operator one time. He was a big part of it all. I hear there was a sort of a falling out. Maybe they needed to grow. You know what he's doing now? Star Wars.

Did the final versions of the films you did with Albert ever surprise you?

No, I was always proud that we realized our dreams. What got to me was that people were like "George, it's time to move on," or said stuff like "Aren't you in a rut?" Sometimes I felt that way, but once I was in it, I was like, "Here we go again." I was able to strut off into new directions and do experimental things.

It sounds like Albert gave you a lot of leeway.

Exactly. I did noir, I did westerns, horror, dance and action. I even did comedy! In my bio, it asked, "What would you like to do that you haven't done?", and I said "I want to do a BEN HUR-esque 70MM Black and White movie."

Your last film with Albert was POSTMORTEM (1999). Did it feel like things were coming to an end?

I didn't realize it was the end. It was just another trip out of the country.

It feels much calmer than Albert's other films. Lots of long steadicam shots.

I think 80-90% was shot on steadicam. Charlie Sheen was there, and he had his mother as his babysitter. After the first day, we never put Charlie first up because he was always late. It had a nice gritty tone, thanks to being set in Glasgow. It seemed to feel right. Anamorphic again. I shot all Fuji stock on that one. That probably gave it a different feel. KNIGHTS was a lot of steadicam, and because we had stunts, it had more cuts to it. I think POSTMORTEM was a single camera for most of the time.

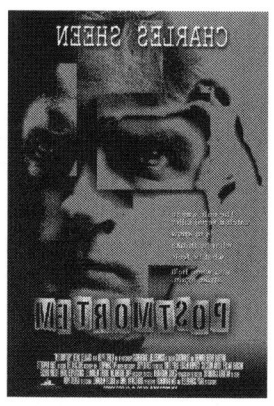

After POSTMORTEM, did you make a conscious decision to find work with different directors?

No, we just organically parted ways. I think Albert was doing me a favour. He was ready for me to go onto other things. Absolutely no hard feelings. It was probably better unspoken...I was hoping something would breakthrough and I always wanted more people to connect with the work... and maybe it held me back... but Louis Morneau discovered me, and it led to another time with him and a few other directors. With Albert, from day one, we were on a similar wavelength. I just wish we had made a genre movie, or a b-movie, that connected. Albert has a voice and a vision, but he didn't want to deal with the layers of control, so a studio would eventually intercede. Even the little bit with Miramax didn't suit him.

Were there any other opportunities to work with Albert?

Philip called me to help out on the green screen thing...

Tales of an Ancient Empire?

Yeah, I came back for a few days like on CAPTAIN AMERICA, and it was great to see Albert. We talked for hours, just catching up, and it was so good. He knew I had grown, and he even said, "George, this is where I am. I'm stuck. I'm not going any further than this. I'm just doing what I can get the money for. You don't need to be here for this." Yeah, it was good to see him. He still had the same long hair!

I think you should be proud of all the great work you did together. There was so much of it!

Yeah, even Richardson and Oliver Stone didn't work as much! Me and Albert worked 23 times together in nine years. I wouldn't have it any other way. Out of that, it made me battle hardened, and as I went on alone, there was nothing I feared.

I imagine nothing is very scary after all of that.

Well, I operated for Abel Ferrara on BODY SNATCHERS (1993).

Wow!

I just did what I had to do. I felt like an equal partner and Abel, and I hashed stuff out. Again, Abel Ferrara didn't phase me. I worked with him again on DANGEROUS GAMES (1993) with Harvey Keitel and Madonna.

After the films you did with Albert, you continued to work in the genre field with Director Louis Morneau…

I think he had seen NEMESIS or some of Albert's movies. He hired me out of the blue and felt honoured he was getting Albert Pyun's DP. We hit it off big time on RETROACTIVE (1997) with Jim Belushi, and that worked out really well. You gotta be three steps ahead of Jim because he's a tough customer.

I assume that relationship with Jim lead to you working on his sitcom ACCORDING TO JIM?

I did three films with Jim! MADE MEN (1999) was a hoot.

I've never seen that one!

That one was so much fun. We used HMI lights without lenses to impress on the audience that the characters were being baked by the sun.

I'll have to check it out *(I did, and it's great!)*

So, Jim Belushi wanted me to do a sitcom, a three camera thing, and I went ,"Are you kidding? No! I want to do art." Jim went, "George, do you want a steady paycheck? Do you want to walk to work, and do you want to see your kids every day?" And I went "Ahhhh... I don't know." I've always been accused by people that my first love was cinema, but finally, I said, "Okay. I might be up for this," and then they wouldn't hire me! The producers said "He's never done this! We have A-list sitcom cinematographers!" I went off to do a movie in Prague, PTERODACTYL (2005) directed by Mark Lester, and I got a call from an executive saying "Fine. We'll let you try, on an episode to episode basis." And Jim said "If he doesn't cut it, I'll fire him!" They said "1. If you don't know something, ask us and 2. If you shoot an un-airable episode, it affects millions." And I didn't really care, which probably helped.

Vilmos Zsigmond did sitcoms too.

I couldn't make heads or tails out of the sitcom style. It's all done from above in a rats nest, but eventually, it became clear to me. I learned to control it and did get nominated for five daytime Emmys over the years.

And your films are finally being released Blu-ray!

Really? Wow. I didn't know that. The lack of good ways to watch the films was really getting to me.

After we had our big screening for producers and investors, that would be the last time people would see it the way it was meant to be seen.

Do you ever want to work as a cinematographer on films again?

I still kind of do. People come to me with scripts, but a lot of the stuff doesn't pan out. There are so many people that want to have their say.

It sounds like on Albert's films, it was really you and him against the world.

Absolutely.

Did you ever get a sense from him that he didn't achieve his visions?

There were probably things going on with the producer back in L.A, but I had no idea about any of that. I think that's why our relationship worked so well on the set. He pushed me, I pushed him, and we'd figure it all out. I can still see him jumping in whenever help was needed. He had no problem carrying a tripod.

It sounds like quite an experience.

We were all really close. I just wish the films had broken through, because it got to the point where I wanted more people to see my work. You know, I told my kids today about your interest in the films I worked on, and they were really proud of me. I still get twinges every now and then about that time, and miss the days where Albert would say "Where do you want to go this year?" and I'd say "How about Mojave?" and then we'd go somewhere beautiful.

SCRIPT NOTES

The following images were provided by Cinematographer George Mooradian and are from his personal scripts.

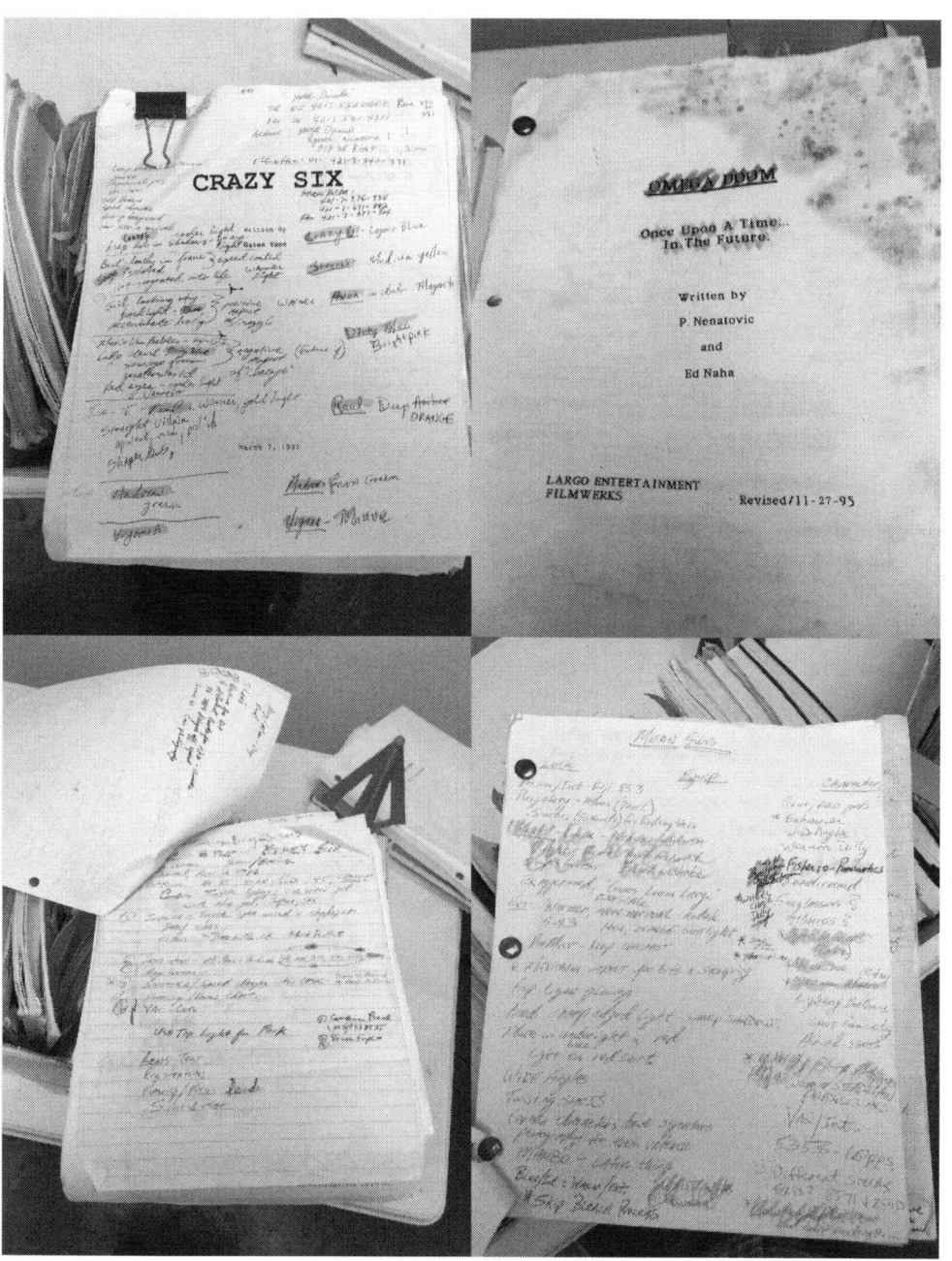

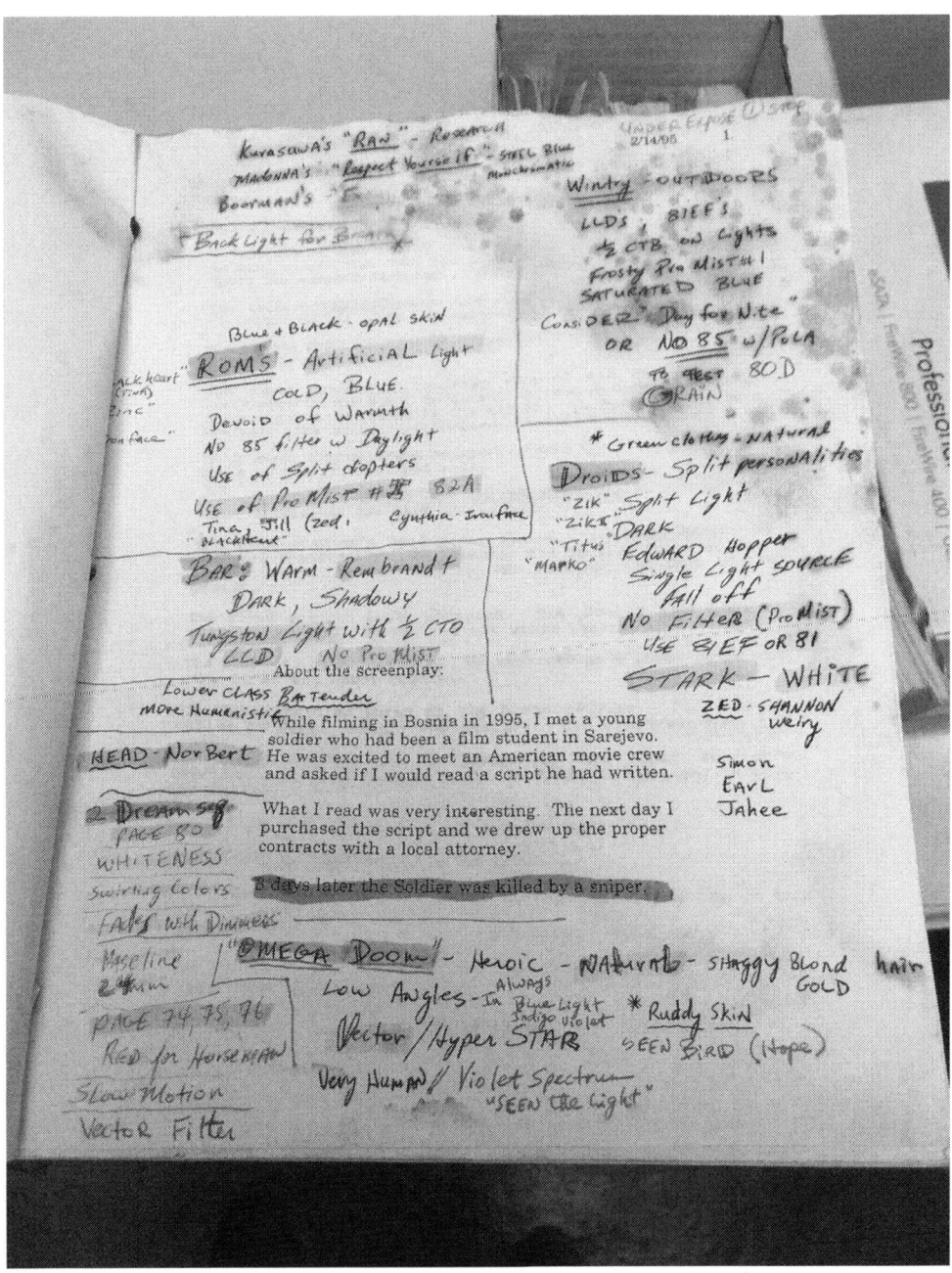

THE WILDERNESS PERIOD

URBAN MENACE (1999) - MAX HAVOC (2004)

The period where Pyun struggled to complete most of his films, let alone make good ones. It includes his infamous URBAN trilogy, a nightmare experience with B-list stars (TICKER) and a major production disaster (MAX HAVOC).

URBAN MENACE (1999)

CAST
Snoop Dogg, Big Pun, Ice-T

WRITERS
Andrew Markell, Tim Story, Albert Pyun (as Hannah Blue)

PRODUCERS
Ice-T, Tom Karnowski, Gary Schmoeller

CINEMATOGRAPHER
Philip Alan Waters

MUSIC
Anthony Riparetti, Ice-T

PRODUCTION DESIGNER
Nenad Pecur

EDITOR
Errin Vasquez

COSTUME DESIGN
Lorraine Alexis, Mahru Toomey

RUNTIME
105 mins

BACK OF THE BOX An insane preacher (Snoop Dog) seeks retribution from the local crime syndicate (headed by Big Pun & Fat Joe) for the violent death of his family and the burning of his church in a horrendous crime spree. An intense action/horror film loaded with explosive action; state of the art visual effects; and a hard-core rap and hip-hop music by Ice-T (from his upcoming Coroner release "7th Deadly Sin).

THE STORY GOES THAT Pyun was supposed to go to Slovakia and make an "Urban Crime" anthology film in 18 days. It wasn't a lot of time, but he had succeeded within tougher constraints in the past.

Instead of the one film, Pyun went to Slovakia and made THREE feature films in 18 days: URBAN MENACE, CORRUPT, and THE WRECKING CREW. Pyun claims the distributor decided to expand the anthology segments to feature length, but I'm not so sure, as "Let's make more movies!" is a classic Pyun motto. He made all three films simultaneously and saved time by reusing the same cast, locations, and camera set-ups. The actors were often unsure what movie they were shooting, but everyone claimed it was an otherwise pleasant experience. The warehouse location was disgusting and freezing, but Pyun remained zen and always seemed to be in control, so the project was able to wrap things up on time and budget.

In URBAN MENACE, Snoop Dogg "stars" as an avenging ghost trapped in a warehouse (which will be a featured location in every URBAN trilogy film). A local gang leader (Big Pun) sends three goons to investigate (led by T.J. Storm). The goons spend the rest of the film walking in circles as Snoop Dogg, or to be more specific, Snoop Dogg's body double, beats them up. The picture runs for a little more than an hour.

For the first time, an Albert Pyun film feels not just incomplete, but wholly untethered from reality. It looks terrible. The dialogue is challenging at best to understand. Freeze frames interrupt conversations. You could argue that some of Pyun's previous productions felt unfinished (VICIOUS LIPS), but none of them have ever veered so drastically off the reservation in style and form as URBAN MENACE. There's a baseline technical expectation when a film is shot on celluloid because the stock, processing and prints are so expensive. That's why even the "worst" bad movies are usually in focus, properly lit, and have audible sound. All of this changed when digital video become viable as an alternative.

Digital cameras took films out of the hands of people with money and put it in the hands of the purely creative. It was a terrific democratic shift that led to a lot of masterpieces, accidental genius and a lot of unwatchable trash by people who had no idea what they were doing. URBAN MENACE was Pyun's first digital film. The lush George Mooradian cinematography is gone, the camera is locked down, and the shots are unimaginative. The post-production team took steps to give the picture a "film look," but they only succeeded in overexposing the image until it turned everything into a blurry mess.

Snoop Dogg was only available to shoot for a few days, so the film does the only thing it can: insert shots of him haphazardly into scenes.

People have a conversation?
CUT TO: Snoop looking through a window.

Characters walk through a hallway?
CUT TO: Snoop staring through a crack in the door.

Snoop gets into a gunfight?
CUT TO: Snoop's death mask is digitally pasted on a stunt doubles' face!

URBAN MENACE comes close to being surreal enough to be entertaining, but its monotonous nature keeps it firmly in the realm of pure frustration. The problem isn't that URBAN was made on the cheap, but that the picture has no engaging style, charm, or energy. Everyone behind the scenes seem entirely lost. What happened to the moodiness of ADRENALIN: FEAR THE RUSH? Or the control of MEAN GUNS? In comparison, Pyun's DECEIT was shot in three days, and it has character, confidence and an appealing visual identity. Noe of that is present here.

Pyun says on the commentary track that all three "Urban" films passed Quality Control for release. I find that difficult to believe.

FUN FACT URBAN MENACE was written by Tim Story who would go to direct BARBERSHOP, FANTASTIC FOUR and RIDE ALONG. I think "written" is probably pretty generous credit in this case.

DOUBLE SAD FACT Of course, nothing is easy, and disaster struck once again on a Pyun production when an airline lost half of the raw footage of the URBAN trilogy while it was being shipped to the states. It sounds like an insurance company may have chipped in a little money for re-shoots, but I doubt it would have been enough to save the pictures. Thankfully, a rough edit of the films had been completed on location, but the quality was terrible and time code had been burnt in on the bottom of the frame. It didn't matter, because it was all they had. Pyun edited in the low quality footage into the release copy and luckily the time code is beyond the

CORRUPT (1999)

CAST
Silkk the Shocker, Ice-T, Tarsha Nicole Jones

WRITER
Andrew Markell

PRODUCERS
Ailawishes, Ice-T, Tom Karnowski, Gary Schmoeller

CINEMATOGRAPHER
Philip Alan Waters

MUSIC
Anthony Riparetti, Ice-T

PRODUCTION DESIGNER
Nenad Pecur

EDITOR
Errin Vasquez

COSTUME DESIGN
Elizabeth Jett

RUNTIME
69 mins

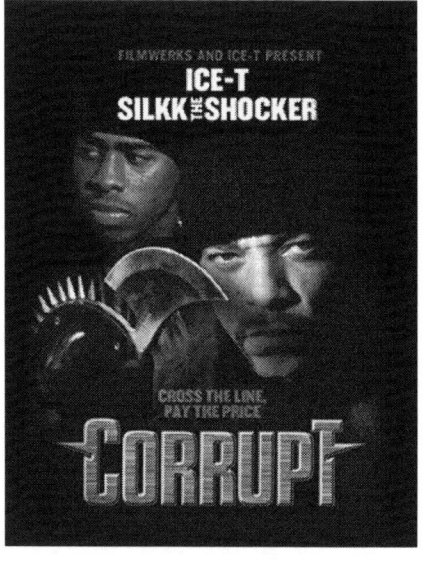

BACK OF THE BOX After decades of terror, two deadly street gangs reach a delicate truce and young MJ (Silkk the Shocker) sees a way out of the hood once and for all. Only Corrupt (Ice-T) stands in MJ's way. Will he make it? Will the truce last? Find out in CORRUPT! Starring Billboard Chart topper and No Limit rap star Silkk The Shocker, Ice-T, Miss Jones, Ernie Hudson Jr., and Karen Dyer. Explosive action and non stop stunts with music by rap master Ice-T from his new Coroner Records release, "7th Deadly Sin".

WHOA. I KINDA LIKED THE SECOND ENTRY IN PYUN'S URBAN TRILOGY?

Okay. I won't go that far. I didn't hate it.

I readied myself for CORRUPT being in the same vein as URBAN MENACE: incomprehensible, static, and filled with eye-searing CGI... but to my surprise, it wasn't any of those things.

Well, it did have an opening where Ice-T lights himself on fire which is brought to life with free AFTER EFFECTS plug-ins, but that's mercilessly the only significant contribution on the CGI front.

I fully expected Ice-T to appear in only a few cutaways, Snoop Dogg style, but he's all over the place in CORRUPT. And he's not even the star! The film is about a woman (Evan La Dare) who would do anything to protect her young brother from bad-guy Ice-T. It would have been easy for La Dare to phone it in, so it's kind of miraculous that she and Ice-T deliver such committed performances in threadbare surroundings that include the Urban Warehouse (TM) and a sitcom level diner set that feels like it was put together by crew members who didn't have a very firm grasp of power tools.

Pyun blew out all the highlights in the cinematography of URBAN MENACE, but here he lets the blocky early-era digital cameras produce colourful images. It gives things a look more akin to the Dogme '95 pictures like Lars Von Trier's (THE IDIOTS) and Thomas Vinterberg's (THE CELEBRATION). The camera even moves!

Of course, CORRUPT has all of the same pacing and editing hiccups of URBAN MENACE, but it's helped immensely by playing things so low-key.

I wouldn't rush out to recommend it because it still feels like a 30-minute short stretched out to an hour, but it does have value as an oddity. After all, it's a poverty row Urban Drama that features an excellent performance by Evan La Darre, gives Ice-T a robust supporting role, and was shot in an ex-Communist country.

FUN FACT

The film's biggest claim to fame is Ice-T's commentary on the DVD. The URBAN trilogy was released at a weird time where it was unimaginable to have a new film released on disc without a commentary track, so CORRUPT has one that features Ernie Hudson Jr. and a second with Ice-T doing his best MST3K shtick.

DOUBLE FUN FACT

I was happy to see star Evan La Darre has had a robust career as a featured player in dozens of video games and prestige television shows. She did voices for the STREET FIGHTER and RESIDENT EVIL games and appeared on the rebooted CHARMED, AGENTS OF SHIELD, and the

THE WRECKING CREW (2000)

CAST
Ice-T, Ernie Hudson Jr., T.J. Storm

WRITER
Albert Pyun (as Hannah Blue)

PRODUCERS
Ice-T, Tom Karnowski, Gary Schmoeller

CINEMATOGRAPHER
Philip Alan Waters

MUSIC
Anthony Riparetti, Ice-T

PRODUCTION DESIGNER
Nenad Pecur

EDITOR
Errin Vasquez

COSTUME DESIGN
(Uncredited)

RUNTIME
80 mins

BACK OF THE BOX A secret high-level government-sponsored hit squad (also known as "The Wrecking Crew") is sent into the mean streets of Chicago to clean up the havoc wreaked by the deadly street gangs. Starring Ice-T as the leader of the hit squad going up against gang bangers Ernie Hudson Jr., T.J Storm and David Askew. News reporter Miss Jones relays the action as audiences watch the city go up in flames. Overlord, Snoop Dogg controls the Hong-Kong style action and martial arts set against the state-of-the-art special effects. Music by hip-hop and rap masters Ice-T from his current Coroner release "7th Deadly Sin."

"THERE WAS NOTHING ALIVE IN THE WAREHOUSES WHERE WE SHOT. NO BIRDS, NO BUGS, NOTHING. I KIND OF LIKE IT THAT WAY."
— ALBERT PYUN

THE WRECKING CREW is the third, and thankfully, the last entry in Pyun's URBAN trilogy.

This time around, a bunch of gangs face off in the Urban Warehouse (TM)s against the titular crew — a group of rogue police officers led by a mostly absent Ice-T. It plays out like a miniature version of MEAN GUNS without any of the character or clever cinematography. THE WRECKING CREW is 60 plus minutes of interchangeable gangsters shooting each other. All the same camera set-ups from the previous films make an appearance. Now and then Ice-T pops up to spit out a one-liner, but it's obvious he was mostly absent, as Pyun uses footage of him from MEAN GUNS to pad things out. It doesn't have the insanity of URBAN MENACE or the earnest drama of CORRUPT, so it's merely a bad action movie.

Snoop Dogg is on the cover, but he only shows up in documentary footage (!) during the film's 10-minute opening credits.

The drop in technical quality from POSTMORTEM to the URBAN trilogy is staggering. One of them is an empty but artfully made rip-off of SILENCE OF THE LAMBS. The other is a static bore seemingly crafted by people with no experience making movies. What happened? Did Pyun accept that making a movie, any movie, was enough?

Perhaps he finally hit the wall that had loomed threateningly on the horizon for years. Pyun kept pulling off projects in a few days, so the production companies must have reasoned, "If he can do it in twelve days, why can't he do it in ten, and if he can do it in ten, why not in five?" Mix that in with the availability of digital camera and computer editing software and there's an unavoidable drop in quality across the board. All those new tools hobbled the films even further until Pyun started to deliver pictures that were so rushed and cheap that people assumed he had always worked in that style.

So, what is the intrinsic value of Pyun's URBAN trilogy?

I can't discuss the way Pyun made his day under challenging conditions. All I can write about (most of the time) is the finished product. It's a tricky thing for me to do when it comes to films like THE WRECKING CREW because by all metrics it's a terrible picture. There's no passion on screen, it's incomprehensible, and there's little to enjoy.

But it is a finished movie.

It did make it to video stores.

People rented it.

Money was made.

Technically, there's nothing wrong with that. The majority of the world work at jobs they don't like. Perhaps the URBAN trilogy paid some medical bills or allowed Pyun to buy a cute stovepipe hat. I don't know! Why should I hold the quality of the films against Pyun? The history of cinema is littered with unfinished projects, so isn't there a victory in completing something? No matter what people might think of it? Even if it changed everything?

The URBAN trilogy would be the last time Pyun would work with his producer, longtime collaborator and childhood friend Tom Karnowski.

Albert's films would never be the same.

FUN FACT IMPERIAL ENTERTAINMENT produced all three films in the URBAN trilogy, yet only THE WRECKING CREW and URBAN MENACE sport the company's name on the back of the DVD case. Both films have a banner that reads "STERLING MILLENNIUM SERIES" on the front cover, but CORRUPT does not, and that's because Lionsgate Entertainment released CORRUPT. The discs were all designed at the same place because all three boxes have the same layout, but CORRUPT is the only one that doesn't have a Pyun commentary track.

TICKER (2001)

CAST
Tom Sizemore, Dennis Hopper, Steven Seagal

WRITERS
Paul B. Margolis, Albert Pyun, Paul Rosenblum

PRODUCER
Ken Aguado

CINEMATOGRAPHER
Philip Alan Waters

MUSIC
Serge Colbert

PRODUCTION DESIGNER
Arnd Stockhausen

EDITORS
Cari Coughlin, Ken Morrisey

COSTUME DESIGN
Tricia Gray

RUNTIME
92 mins

BACK OF THE BOX When a mad bomber (Dennis Hopper) descends on San Francisco, it's up to two men to uncover his plot and find the massive bomb hidden somewhere in the city. Steven Seagal stars as the Zen leader of the bomb squad and Tom Sizemore is a vice cop out for vengeance. Featuring special appearance by pop sensation Chili.

I WROTE THE FOLLOWING AFTER I SAW TICKER FOR THE FIRST TIME:

"An entire film composed of actors spouting auto-translated dialogue in disconnected close-ups. Pyun at his most Eisensteinian. Lots of good slow-motion explosions."

I didn't know the half of it.

On the surface, TICKER is another lacklustre direct-to-video Steven Seagal film. Tom Sizemore stars as a vice cop out for revenge against a mad bomber who killed his family. Steven Seagal is an explosive expert who loves to spout nonsense. Dennis Hopper is an IRA terrorist. Everyone looks somewhat bored, but there's still stuff to enjoy: terrible green screens, Hopper's disappearing and reappearing Irish accent, and Seagal's mumbled zen mysticisms are all good for a laugh. It is bereft of action, but it does the job.

On the positive side of things, it's refreshing to see Pyun work with a budget again. He gets to make something with scope, film a few great explosions, and work with a cast of recognizable faces. Jaime Pressly makes an appearance. Rapper Nas plays a cop named Fuzzy (yes, really). Pyun Players Norbert Weisser and Michael Halsey show up in sizable roles. It's disjointed, but still stands head and shoulders above other Seagal stinkers like OUT OF REACH and TOMORROW YOU DIE.

TICKER seemed to be an indication Pyun was taking a step toward getting the kind of budgets he used to work with back in the glory days of Cannon and KICKBOXER 2.

That is until you peel TICKER's skin away to reveal the surgically scarred monstrosity beneath.

The film was shot in 12 days.

Every explosion, big stunt and establishing shot is stock footage from other NU IMAGE productions. Dennis Hopper was only on set for a single day. Steven Seagal worked for six days. Tom Sizemore shares the frame with Seagal in only one scene. The rest of the time, they were filmed separately. The camera is so tight on Seagal all the time because he's alone in a warehouse reading his dialogue up against a black cloth, and then through the magic of editing, he's inserted into the film with the rest of the cast.

The cost-cutting doesn't end there either. For example, there's a nice looking shot of Dennis Hopper walking down a hallway, but on the commentary track the producer points out it's from another NU IMAGE film called THE LAST DAYS OF FRANKIE THE FLY. That shot is the background of the TICKER DVD menu!

On the one hand, it's incredible that Pyun was able to put together anything releasable within those limitations.

On the other, it's another step toward Pyun's sad exit from the world of Hollywood film making.

FUN FACT Seagal had a very brief career resurgence thanks to his film EXIT WOUNDS (2001) making money, but then he followed it up TICKER, and his last starring role in a theatrically released project was the hilariously inept HALF PAST DEAD (2002) - which was directed by early Pyun Player Don Michael Paul! After that, Seagal was banished to the world of DTV forever, where he continues to sit in chairs, mumble, and refuse to dub his own voice. The definitive essay on TICKER can be found in the fantastic book SEAGALOGY: A STUDY OF THE ASS-KICKING FILMS OF STEVEN SEAGAL by Vern.

DOUBLE FUN FACT The DVD commentary for TICKER is surreal. It's mostly silent, but every now and then Pyun and the producer chime to say how nice the entire cast was - especially Seagal. It sounds like a kidnapper

BAD BIZNESS (2003)

DIRECTORS
Jim Wynorski (as Bob E. Brown), Albert Pyun (uncredited)

CAST
Traci Bingham, Master P, Brent Huff

WRITER
Sean McGinly

PRODUCERS
Christopher Bates, Hugh Jordan, Albert Pyun, Jim Valdez

CINEMATOGRAPHER
Ted Caloroso

MUSIC
(Uncredited)

PRODUCTION DESIGNER
(Uncredited)

EDITOR
Thomas Main

COSTUME DESIGN
Cindy Renaud-Kim

RUNTIME
91 mins

BACK OF THE BOX As the weather gets hotter, bodies of girls start showing up dead... one by one. A beautiful cop gets pulled into the dark underworld of prostitution when she finds out that the common tie between all the victims is a call girl ring. When one mysterious power player in the city tries to keep the murders under wraps, she has only one chance left to catch the killer... and her suspect is closer than she thinks.

"BREASTS ARE THE CHEAPEST SPECIAL EFFECT IN THE BUSINESS."
— JIM WYNORSKI

Technically, this is not an Albert Pyun film. Based on what little information I could find, Pyun only worked on the picture for a few days before being fired and replaced by director Jim Wynorski (who took the pseudonym Bob E. Brown.)

The end product features only one of Pyun's signatures: the appearance of actor Norbert Weisser, who appears throughout the film but seems to have shot all of his material in a single day behind a desk. The rest of the picture is classic Jim Wynorski: soft-focus shenanigans packed with naked breasts, lesbian make-out sessions, and more breasts.

The plot involves a hotel security guard (ex-BAYWATCH star Sandra Marshall) hunting down a serial killer who's murdering busty women. There's no excitement, action, gore, creativity, or fun on display. Rapper Master P appears by himself in a few scenes filmed in a hotel room. He has no impact on the plot, but he's on the cover. The film is a slog for everyone who isn't a 12-year old boy without the internet.

Jim Wynorski's career makes for an interesting parallel to Pyun's. Both of them got into the industry because they loved movies. Wynorski's started as the marketing director for Roger Corman's New World Pictures and wrote screenplays for Jack Hill's SORCERESS (1982) and the teen sex romp SCREWBALLS (1983). Jim's first directorial effort was an independent production called THE LOST EMPIRE (1984), and like Pyun's SWORD AND THE SORCERER, Wynorski filled his debut with everything he loved. It's got martial arts, niche pop cultural references, beautiful women, ninjas, and a man in a gorilla suit. From there, Wynorski bounced around as a director, but mostly stuck by his old boss Roger Corman. His notable films include the entertaining killer-robots slasher CHOPPING MALL (1986), the goofy meta sequel DEATHSTALKER II (1987), and the playful superhero pastiche RETURN OF SWAMP THING (1989).

The critical difference between Wynorski and Pyun is that when the bottom of the industry fell out, Pyun was sent out to pasture, while Wynorski soldiered on thanks to his one great love: naked women. Wynorski was more than happy to deliver films that were nothing more than an excuse for T&A. The sense of fun in his early work evaporated, but he was able to continue to write/direct/produce films through the 2000s with titles like THE WITCHES OF BREASTWICK, BUSTY COPS 2, and HOUSE ON HOOTER HILL. He shot them all in 3-5 days.

Eventually, his audience realized they could see as many naked people as they wanted online and Wynorski's output slowed until a new muse came calling... television! Wynorski has been able to stay in business thanks to a steady stream of CGI-filled monster movies (COBRAGATOR) and family-friendly material (A DOGGONE CHRISTMAS).

For a closer look at Wynorski and his process, I highly recommend the fantastic documentary POPATOPOLIS (2009).

MAX HAVOC: CURSE OF THE DRAGON (2004)

DIRECTORS
Albert Pyun, Isaac Florentine (co-director)

CAST
Mickey Hardt, Nikki Ziering, Scott L. Schwartz

WRITER
Irina Mishina

PRODUCERS
Melissa Ciampa, Connie Dolphin

CINEMATOGRAPHER
Ted Caloroso

MUSIC
Richard Friedman

PRODUCTION DESIGNER
(Uncredited)

EDITOR
Irit Raz

COSTUME DESIGN
Collette Jones

RUNTIME
90 mins

BACK OF THE BOX Max Havoc (Mickey Hardt) has forsaken his life as a former world kickboxing champion to redefine himself as a sports photographer. After being advised to take a simple assignment in Guam by his agent Joe (Diego Wallraff), he meets up with his old friend and former trainer Tahsi (Richard Roundtree) to shoot an ad campaign. After arriving in Guam, Max meets two sisters, Jane (Joanna Krupa) and Christy Goody (Tawny Sablan), after he rescues the younger sister from drowning. Max's simple assignment takes a dark turn as he learns that the rogue warriors, the Black Dragons, will stop at nothing to reclaim a sacred burial urn which was purchased by Jane from Tahsi. Only Max has the strength and smarts to restore the Jade Dragon to its rightful owner.

MAX HAVOC WAS THE LAST TIME PYUN WORKED WITH A BIG CREW.

It was also the last time he would shoot on film.

And it would be the last time he was fired from a production.

It's a real shame that MAX HAVOC was Pyun's studio swan song. One would have hoped Pyun could have burned all his bridges in the name of a mad RADIOACTIVE DREAMS-like passion project. Sadly, MAX HAVOC is simply a disposable action film with a bland lead and a forgettable premise. The concept had supposedly been floating around for a decade, which I find hilarious because all Max Havoc does is take photos and fight! Why were producers chomping at the bit to bring him to the screen? Mickey Hardt may be a great Swiss actor, but he's dead weight as a lead saddled with way too much dialogue. For a guy named Havoc, he doesn't create much.

Like a lot of late-period Pyun films (BAD BIZNESS), most of the picture takes place in and around a hotel. There's a lot of footage of people riding around on jet skis. The Pyun shot action is average, and it's obvious he only got the bare bones of what was needed. Ace fight choreographer J.J. Perry (JOHN WICK 2) does what he can with the material, but the flat camera angles don't do his work any favours.

If there's one thing that people remember about MAX HAVOC, it's the controversy that followed in its wake. The film was shot on the island of Guam, and the producers promised the government an influx of cash and tourism, which prompted Guam to invest $800,000 into the production. The details of what went wrong are complicated, and there are many articles out there on the subject, so let's just say it ended in disaster, and everyone left pissed off and litigious.

Back in Hollywood, Millennium Films saw Albert Pyun's cut of MAX HAVOC and fired him. In an attempt to salvage the project, the company brought in director Isaac Florentine to finish the job. Florentine shot for ten extra days in LA. He added a bunch of decent fight scenes set in a dark warehouse, fleshed out Max's back story, and added Richard Roundtree and David Carradine to the cast. It didn't make the film good, but it did slightly improve it.

I love Pyun and Florentine. Pyun is weird and messy. Florentine is direct and lean. I discovered both of them on the same day when I bought Pyun's MEAN GUNS and Florentine's U.S. SEALS II on DVD at HMV. Born in Israel, Florentine got

into the industry with an award-winning short and transitioned into working as a fight choreographer before getting his shot to direct his first feature, DESERT KICKBOXER (1992). From there, he cut his teeth putting together the action scenes for the original MIGHTY MORPHING POWER RANGERS series (1993-1994) and honed his directorial skills on direct-to-video features like HIGH VOLTAGE (1998), COLD HARVEST (1999) and BRIDGE OF THE DRAGONS (1999).

The great thing about Florentine is that he has a very distinct visual style: clean, energetic, and in love with a camera that is always moving in exciting ways. A fan can watch a Florentine shot fight scene and instantly know he was involved. And unlike many DTV action directors, Florentine genuinely loves making action movies and always pushes the material above and beyond. He's made little gems like U.S. SEALS II (an insane martial art siege picture), introduced Scott Adkins to the world with SPECIAL FORCES (2003) and gained a lot of critical attention with his fantastic entries in the UNDISPUTED and NINJA franchises.

Sadly, Florentine still hasn't had a chance to move on to bigger budgeted productions and is still sweating it out in the DTV trenches.

FUN FACT A sequel to CURSE OF THE DRAGON was made called MAX HAVOC: RING OF FIRE (2006). It was meant to lead into a TV series, but never did, because no one cared.

PYUN MISCELLANEA
WHERE DID THE "F" IN ALBERT PYUN GO?

Albert Pyun was credited as Albert F. Pyun on his second and third films but dropped the middle initial from DOWN TWISTED onward. I found a file from America's 1940 census that lists a ten-year-old boy named Albert Pyun born in Honolulu, Hawaii from Korean parents. The boy's date of birth is listed as 1930, so unless the subject of this book is a shape shifting vampire or Albert Pyun is a common Hawaiian name, my guess is that the one listed on the census is the director's father. Albert the Filmmaker may have asked to be credited as Albert F. Pyun early on to distinguish himself from his father, but realized by DOWN TWISTED that it wouldn't be an issue. The Writer/Director Albert Pyun has always identified as Hawaiian and has never spoken of his Korean heritage.

To muddy the waters even further, producer Thom Karnowski also put an F. in his name on the credits of VICIOUS LIPS, so perhaps the letter is only there to indicate both of their frustration on the two difficult productions.

PYUN'S FIRST FEATURE: DRAGONS (1974)

The only reference to this unavailable film I've come across was in a post on Albert Pyun's blog dated 8/25/2015. "Here I am working on my feature film called DRAGONS in 1974. It starred Jim Emmerson. This shoot was done in secret at Loyola Marymount using their equipment." Albert goes on to describe the project's crew, which included Tom Karnowski (pictured with long blond hair) and he says that the film was about a scrawny kid who idolized Bruce Lee. They had to show the feature to Lee's widow, Linda Lee, to get permission to use her husband's image. I assume DRAGONS was never properly completed, because there's no other traces of it I could find.

TELEVISION PYUN: THE FIFTH CORNER (1992)

Albert has mentioned he worked as a commercial film editor at KGMB in Honolulu and worked for agencies such as Bozell Jacobs and Leo Burnett, but his only other TV credit as a director is for the second episode of short-lived NBC series THE FIFTH CORNER (1992). The show starred Alex McArthur as a man who wakes up one morning suffering amnesia. He comes to believe he's a spy, so he goes on the run and is pursued by all sorts of nefarious people (like a slumming James Coburn). Six episodes of the series were produced.

I was able to hunt down the episode Pyun directed ("Eva") and the show revealed itself to be a hyper-stylized neo-noir that packs a hundred twists into its forty-seven-minute frame. The protagonist is arrested for the murder of a Japanese man, is threatened with being extradited (by an uncredited Thom Mathews), taken back into custody by an uncredited Brion James, and helped by guitar slinging

Tim Thomerson (who is credited!). Mädchen Amick (TWIN PEAKS) shows up in a supporting role. It's difficult to see what Pyun brought to the table that wasn't already set-up in the pilot, beyond his stable of actors and a climatic martial arts fight scene, which makes his brush with television merely a curiosity.

THE UNFINISHED FILM: SORCERERS (1997)

Stars: Simon Clarke, Kenzie Phillips, Nathan Ferrier
Writers: Cynthia Curnan, Randall Fontana
Producers: Tom Karnowski, Teri Blythe, Michael Su
Cinematographer: George Mooradian
Editor: Albert Pyun
Music: Anthony Riparetti
Costume Design: Shirley Kurata
Production Design: (uncredited)
Runtime: 100 mins

BACK OF THE BOX Sorcerers is an unfinished animated fantasy film that would have combined live actors with CG backgrounds and characters in a story inspired by The Three Musketeers by Alexander Dumas.

Pyun shot SORCERERS entirely on greenscreens in 1997, but never completed the film after the cost of implementing the computer generated imagery proved to be too costly.

In July 2006, a YouTuber user called obscurecultmovies, who I assume is a pseudonym for Albert or his partner Cynthia Curnan, released the first 10 mins of the film split into three parts and noted that "The film would have been made up of 36 episodes, all of which were shot.

The clips are very brief, but they seem to indicate the film would have been a fantasy/sci-fi mash-up in the same sprawling mode as TALES OF AN ANCIENT EMPIRE (2010).

SORCERERS has been mentioned sporadically by Pyun and Curnan over the years, and the inclusion of actors like Tommie Vegas in the current IMDB cast list (she acted in Pyun's last released film) would lead me to believe that more shooting has been completed, but nothing new has yet to be released.

FILMWERKS (1994-2005)

Filmwerks is a company Albert Pyun helped start in an attempt to gain more control over the production and release of his films (à la Roger Corman) Filmwerks was associated with seventeen films directed by Albert. The last one to sport the company's logo was INVASION (2005).

PYUN THE PRODUCER

Surprisingly, Pyun has only four credits as a feature film producer: BLOODMATCH (1989), TICKER (2001), FINAL EXAMINATION (2002), and BAD BIZNESS (2003). All his other films were principally produced by Tom Karnowski and Gary Schmoeller. The fact that Pyun is credited as a producer on TICKER and BAD BIZNESS probably has something to do with the difficulty he had on those productions. His outlier producer credit is on FINAL EXAMINATION. Albert didn't direct the film, but he did work on the film's twin BAD BIZNESS. Both films are set in Hawaii, have a serial killer knocking off large breasted women, and feature actor Brent Huff. The pictures were produced by Epsilon Motion Pictures and were shot in 2003, but only FINAL EXAMINATION

was produced by 'Hawaii Filmwerks' (The company's only credit). The director of FINAL EXAMINATION is Fred Olen Ray (credited as Ed Raymond) a good friend of BAD BIZNESS director Jim Wynorski, as they served as the co-directors on DINOSAUR ISLAND (1994) and SCREAM QUEEN HOT TUB PARTY (1991). Did Fred Olen Ray get brought on after Jim Wynorski took over BAD BIZNESS? Or did Fred suggest Jim pick up the slack on BIZNESS after Albert left? It's a mystery no one is desperate to solve!

THE JAPANESE CUTS

Alternative versions of NEMESIS (1992) and RADIOACTIVE DREAMS (1985) have both appeared on Japanese laserdisc. The new cuts feature more scenes, alternate shots, and extra violence. I'm unsure of how closely Pyun was involved with them, but if I had to take a guess, I'd say they were earlier edits. The Japanese cut of NEMESIS features extended scenes, a little more action, and the deletion of the final stop motion exo-skeleton fight to make way for a different ending.

The Japanese edit of RADIOACTIVE DREAMS plays like a workprint where every scene was included. It gives things more of a chance to breathe, but by consequence, the new moments make the picture more tonally inconsistent and slower paced. In the Japanese edit, a radio DJ named Nikki Nuker does voice-over throughout, Michael Dudikoff is angrier, and a major character, who disappears from the theatrical release, is killed on-screen

Personally, I found a lot of the additions diluted the film's emotional through line and I believe it was the right decision to delete them. I doubt Pyun prefers the Japanese cut because it removes the giant rat creature from the film and makes the final musical number feel like a dream sequence.

THE FREEDOM PERIOD

INVASION (2005) - PRESENT DAY

Pyun has always been an independent operator, but in this period he truly went off to do his own thing. It includes his most bold experiments (INVASION), revisionist genre outings (LEFT FOR DEAD) and crushing defeats (ABELAR: TALES OF AN ANCIENT EMPIRE).

INVASION
(AKA INFECTION)
(2005)

CAST
Jenny Dare Paulin, Morgan Weisser, Alan Abelew

WRITER
Cynthia Curnan

PRODUCERS
Rob Ladesich, Norbert Weisser

CINEMATOGRAPHER
Jim Hagopian

MUSIC
Anthony Riparetti

PRODUCTION DESIGNER
(Uncredited)

EDITORS
Chris Burkhalter,
Ken Morrisey

COSTUME DESIGN
Tricia Gray

RUNTIME
81 mins

BACK OF THE BOX Prolific B-movie director Albert Pyun (Dollman, Omega Doom) takes the reigns for this tale of a small town overtaken by a highly contagious alien plague on the night of the senior prom. As the local teens party their way through prom night, a meteor crashes to the earth in a small California town, rattling Lawton rancher Larry Jenkins. When Larry puts a call in to the local police, Inspector Bardo is immediately dispatched to investigate. Upon arriving on the scene, Inspector Bardo is terrified to find that a horrific alien virus has infected the unsuspecting Jenkins. Before he can react, Inspector Bardo is savagely attacked by the rampaging rancher. Now, as the two unwitting hosts make their way into Lawton while viciously attacking and contaminating everyone in their path, adolescent lovebirds Cheryl and Timmy sit perched high atop Lover's Lane completely unaware of the approaching terror. When Timmy is infected, Cheryl is left to fend for herself in the darkened forest. Perhaps if Cheryl can make it to the authorities in time, she can prevent the infection from spreading to L.A.

IF YOU WATCH the Albert Pyun films leading up to INVASION, you can see every production get progressively more impoverished until there's nothing left up on the screen. After MAX HAVOC, most directors would have called it quits. Pyun had a good run. He made 40 films. Would it be so wrong if he spent the rest of his days working as a film school teacher at a small college?

Impossible! Albert Pyun wouldn't be Albert Pyun if he quit making movies! It's the only thing that keeps him going! But how does one make a film when you have no money or time?

You make a "one long take" found footage film of course!

INVASION does have a nifty gimmick: the entire picture was filmed from a car's dashboard cam as it rolls along a dark forest hill road. The film has an eerie atmosphere, some decent jump scares, and would probably be pretty effective in a dark theatre... for the first half-hour. Tedium does eventually set in. There's only so long an audience can stare at the same dirt road lit by headlights.

If I had liked the characters, it could have worked, but the leads are the same whiny screamers that THE BLAIR WITCH turned into found footage staples. I don't hate the found footage "genre" because it's technically a  stylistic template, but it's undeniable that tropes like unlikeable characters, endless chatter, and go-nowhere endings (everyone dies) are the norm. INVASION may have felt fresher at the time of its release, but watched today, it plays like every other found footage horror picture you'd stumble on in the Netflix graveyard. Pyun spoke at the time that he was happy to be out of the Hollywood system. Now, he didn't have to worry if something was commercially viable in every world market, and for the first time as a film director, he was utterly in control. No one could touch one frame if he didn't want them too — but they could change the title. INVASION was initially called INFESTATION, and the distributor switched it. Albert could never win!

INVASION'S bold experimentation makes me wish Albert could have pursued his craft into even odder art house territory and ditched the genre projects. A lot of my misgivings with his latter day period stems from the fact that he doesn't have the resources to deliver what his projects promise. That would not be an issue if he made a psychodrama. Give me Pyun's PERSONA!

FUN FACT Albert Pyun claims the film was shot in one take, and they did capture the film in chronological order, but the full-frame white flashes that appear throughout the picture lead me to believe a few takes may have been stitched together.

COOL AIR (2006)

CAST
Morgan Weisser, Crystal Laws Green, Jenny Dare Paulin

WRITERS
Cynthia Curnan (adaptation), H.P. Lovecraft (short story)

PRODUCERS
Rob Ladesich, Norbert Weisser

CINEMATOGRAPHER
Jim Hagopian

MUSIC
Anthony Riparetti

PRODUCTION DESIGNER
(Uncredited)

EDITOR
Glen Berry

COSTUME DESIGN
Tricia Gray

RUNTIME
78 mins

BACK OF THE BOX A screenwriter wrestling with creative block is confronted with unimaginable evil after suffering a heart attack, and being saved by the mysterious doctor who lives in an upstairs apartment.

COOL AIR is an H.P. Lovecraft short story about a young man in a boarding house who discovers that his upstairs neighbour is a dead scientist. The scientist has dodged the reaper thanks to the help of a refrigerated apartment. In the end, the scientist melts. That's it!

In Pyun's version of COOL AIR, the protagonist (Morgan Weisser, son of Pyun All-Star Norbert) is a Hollywood screenwriter suffering writer's block. He moves into a house situated in the desert with borders that include a mentally disabled young woman (Jenny Dare Paulin), a Disney animator (Norbert Weisser), and a mysterious doctor (Crystal Laws Green). The screenwriter has a heart attack, and it's only thanks to the help of the Doctor he lives. Or is he already dead?

I know it's in the public domain, but I've always been mystified why Lovecraft's COOL AIR keeps getting adapted. There isn't much to it beyond the final gruesome twist. Notable versions include a comic illustrated by Bernie Wrightson for EERIE (1975), an episode of NIGHT GALLERY (1971), and a segment in the Lovecraft anthology film NECRONOMICON (1994) by Japanese director Shusuke Kaneko - which is the only adaption, to my knowledge, that delivers a big gooey meltdown climax.

In his version, Pyun has a unique desert setting (which includes a lot of menacing goats), but he never plays up any of the horror, and he can't commit to any big special effects due to budget limitations, so the film desperately struggles to find a reason to exist.

COOL AIR is a home movie. It's got a lot of friendly faces, a cheap look, and zero drive. I'm sure that everyone involved had a swell time, but like the YouTube video of your friend's vacation, there's nothing of any interest for people that weren't there.

Pyun seems weighed down by the digital nature of the production. His natural visual flair is absent and is replaced by a locked-down shooting style which makes it look like one of David Decoteau's "tighty whitey" films (A TALKING CAT!?!). Cynthia Curnan's script tries to bring something new to the table by implementing hard-boiled SUNSET BOULEVARD style narration along with a new-age mysticism slant to the story, but it just doesn't work for me. In the end, it's a zero-budget product that doesn't commit to the most basic horror tropes and fails to deliver the climax of its source material.

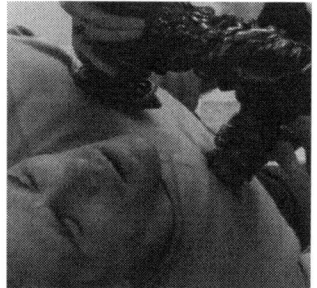

Was all of Pyun's energy sucked out by the digital equipment? Was his golden age style inherently intertwined with his colleagues from the 90s? Or is COOL AIR merely the work of an artist who wanted to try something radically different and stumbled along the way.

LEFT FOR DEAD (2007)

CAST
Victoria Maurette, Soledad Arocena, Andres Bagg

WRITER
Chad Leslie

PRODUCERS
Michael Najjar, Gary Schmoeller

CINEMATOGRAPHER
Alejandro Millán

MUSIC
Anthony Riparetti

PRODUCTION DESIGNERS
Sabrina Suarez, Florencia Della Vedova

EDITOR
Ken Morrisey

COSTUME DESIGN
Laura Aguerrebehere, Mariana Ravioli

RUNTIME
84 mins

BACK OF THE BOX The west goes gruesome in this gunslinging terror ride into the town of Amnesty. The small town is a shattered shell of a place, empty of all life except Mobius, a vengeful killer who cuts down anyone unfortunate enough to cross his path. But Clem is coming to town - and she and her posse are not going to go quietly.

IF YOU DON'T LIKE Albert Pyun's late-period stylistic choices run for the hills. LEFT FOR DEAD is a supernatural Spaghetti Western filled with weird freeze frames, dodgy CGI, and baffling storytelling choices, but this time around, it all worked for me!

Clementine Templeton (Victoria Maurette) is a mean gunslinger who has a bone to pick with the world. She teams up with a gang of prostitutes to hunt down a cowardly man who impregnated one of them, and the chase leads the women to an abandoned ghost town called "Amnesty" where an immortal Satan powered killer (Andres Bagg) starts to pick them off one by one in gruesome (and budget-conscious) ways.

LEFT FOR DEAD was shot in eleven days in Argentina (a first and last for Pyun), and the support of the local technical team seems to have helped the project immensely. The film has a digital sheen, but it feels textured. Everyone is covered in dirt. The costumes are worn. The visuals are sweaty. It's got the look of the great Eurowesterns of the late '60s mixed in with the "long lens style" that would come to dominate Pyun's freedom period. The fact that it's shot on a real location definitely makes a difference.

I was worried when the film started with a bunch of explanatory title cards (My pet peeve), but after that things settled into a rhythm. I found that the cast of local Argentinian actors brought a different flavour to the proceedings. The story's emotional journey is complicated in its shading but reasonably straightforward in its execution: a woman wants revenge, she ends up in a siege situation, and she has to come to terms with what her revenge would entail. It's simple, direct, but never obvious. I should also note that Tony Riparetti's sound design and music for the picture are excellent. He packs every cut with a crackling whoosh, and his Morricone inflected score is memorable without feeling like a rip-off.

The film could have done with one more pass of edits, especially to remove a silly CGI skull in the last shot, but overall, Pyun succeeds in what he set out to do. LEFT FOR DEAD won't be for everyone, because the film does look cheap, but the open-minded will find something to enjoy. Or be entirely baffled. It could go either way.

NOT A FUN FACT BUT AN OBSERVATION

All of Pyun's late-period films (and his director's cuts) start with multiple title cards that overcomplicates things to the extreme. Personally, I'd much rather wonder what's going on than have it confusingly explained. I can only assume they became a bad habit because Pyun spent an entire career hearing people go "Your films are too weird!" and the cards are his attempt to make things clearer.

ROAD TO HELL (2008)

CAST
Michael Paré, Clare Kramer, Courtney Peldon

WRITER
Cynthia Curnan

PRODUCER
Sazzy Lee Calhoun

CINEMATOGRAPHERS
Jim Hagopian,
Michael Su

MUSIC
Anthony Riparetti

PRODUCTION DESIGNER
Norman Greenwood

EDITORS
Chiba & Nobu
(Albert Pyun's Dogs)
Daniel Ray

COSTUME DESIGN
Susan Doepner-Senac,
Olwen Zarlengo

RUNTIME
87 mins

BACK OF THE BOX Inspired by Walter Hill's 1984 classic STREETS OF FIRE - a soldier who has been fighting a long war is driven mad because he no longer believes in any purpose or righteous truth behind the killing. He comes home to a surreal world looking for his first and only love from his youth, believing she will rescue him from his demons. On the road to edge city he encounters two seductive spree killers who oppose his efforts to find his love and redemption he desperately seeks.

WALTER HILL'S rock 'n' roll fable STREETS OF FIRE (1984) is a film I like, but wish I loved. The 1984 box office flop is the tale of cool dude Tom Cody (Michael Paré) going on a one crazy night adventure to save his former lover (Diane Lane) from an evil William Dafoe. The film is hyper-stylized (everything was shot on a giant backlot), has fantastic songs by Jim Steinman, and is a flawed piece of work that I have difficulty connecting with. The entire production feels locked in stasis. All of the elements are present, but it never gets a chance to explode (beyond its incredible music numbers). It makes sense that Pyun would be a mega fan. Every one of his early films (RADIOACTIVE DREAMS, VICIOUS LIPS, and even SPITFIRE) could be described as working off Walter Hill's rock 'n' roll movie template.

But I never expected Pyun to make an unofficial sequel to STREETS OF FIRE.

Pyun said the project came about when he and his creative collaborator Cynthia Curnan had different interpretations of where Tom Cody ended up after the credits of STREETS. Pyun saw the ending as romantic, Curnan thought it was tragic. So, she wrote a script to articulate her position, and Pyun decided to make it. They convinced Michael Paré to return as Tom Cody, grabbed a cameo from Cody's on-screen sister and Pyun player Deborah Van Valkenburgh, and even scored permission to do covers of Jim Steinman's great songs from the original. The final result is one hell of a bad trip (literally and

figuratively). Michael Paré's Tom Cody is introduced (20 minutes in) as a broken man who has already tortured and killed several innocent people. All he wants to do is see his old flame Ellen again, but he's trapped in a hellish unending desert. Cody runs into two spree killers (Clare Kramer and Courtney Peldon) which leads to torture and more murder. Eventually, Cody ends up at his daughter's (Roxy Gunn) concert. He listens to her perform three songs (which include two Jim Steinman covers) and the movie finishes with a title card that wraps things up in a cute unearned bow. Did I mention that it's mostly shot on a green screen? And that the archangel Gabriel narrates the proceedings? And everyone is trapped in limbo? I think? The film's themes are so muddled that I had no idea what it was trying to say in the end. Did Tom Cody leave his evil way of life by helping murder two murderers? Is he dead? Are they all dead?

It's impossible for me to articulate the batshit craziness of ROAD TO HELL. Not since URBAN MENACE have I struggled so mightily to figure out what was going on in Albert Pyun's mind. The film looks like SIN CITY on acid. There are random freeze frames, disconnected interviews, and head-scratching cutaways. Pyun obviously idolizes the original picture, but his take on the material is incredibly noxious. Maybe he was trying to articulate that an anti-hero like Tom Cody was doomed to be an awful person in real life? It's a miserable experience, but perhaps that's the point?

The whole thing is akin to thinking about STREETS OF FIRE right before going to sleep and having the iconography crash into your nightmares until it's all muddled together into one big stew of pure discomfort.

FUN FACT The film's listed as being shot in 2008, and it did screen in 2012 at a few festivals, but due to several post-production and distributions issues, it wasn't properly released until 2017

BULLETFACE (2010)

DIRECTOR
Albert Pyun

CAST
Victoria Maurette, Steven Bauer, Morgan Weisser

WRITER
Randall Fontana

PRODUCERS
Nelson Carpentier, Joe Baile, Rob Ladesich, Sazzy Lee Calhoun, Michael Najjar, Gary Schmoeller

CINEMATOGRAPHERS
Jim Hagopian, Michael Kutcher

MUSIC
Anthony Riparetti

PRODUCTION DESIGNER
Alex Cassun

EDITOR
Ken Morrisey

COSTUME DESIGN
Glenda Maddox

RUNTIME
82 mins

BACK OF THE BOX Horror and Revenge drive this thriller set in the sex and human trafficking underbelly of a nightmarish city where spinal fluid has become the drug of choice... with frightening consequences. The story is set along the Mexico/California Border, principally in Imperial Beach, CA. It concerns a female DEA agent, who in protecting her petty criminal younger brother, gets herself arrested and imprisoned in a nightmarish penal colony. While she's in prison her brother is murdered by a drug dealer who's creating a new DNA-altering drug made from human spinal fluid... tapped from the living. A rogue FBI agent bribes the prison officials to let Dara out to avenge her brother's murder as well as bring down the drug lord in ways the Feds cannot. The catch? She only gets 60-hours get-out-of-jail free card and must return to the prison to serve out her 20-year sentence, or the FBI agent, who got her out, must take her place.

"I WANTED TO MAKE A MONOGRAM NOIR."
— ALBERT PYUN

Monogram was a Poverty Row production company that operated out of Los Angeles in the '40s. It would churn out hour-long comedies, horror films, noirs, and whatever else was popular at the time. The films were shot in a few days, given a lurid poster, and attached to the bottom of double and triple bills in what was known as "block booking." If the theatres wanted to play a distributor's big pictures, they had to accept everything that was offered. They paid a flat fee for the Poverty Row product, so it didn't make a difference if the films were successful or good, because profit wasn't part of the equation. In the late '40s, the studios were hit with an antitrust case, and block booking

was deemed an illegal activity. With their revenue stream cut off, most of the Poverty Row studios were forced to shut down.

There's something intoxicating about a production company giving a director a little money, very little time, and barely any resources to shoot something, anything, that was guaranteed to have an audience (willing or otherwise). It leads a hopeful mind to imagine that great auteurs would flourish in that kind of environment.

Nope.

Poverty Row studios like Monogram wasn't interested in artists. They wanted technicians who could deliver something on time and budget. Most Poverty Row directors were people like William "One Shot" Beaudine (BELA LUGOSI MEETS A BROOKLYN GORILLA), who was a journeyman in the silent days of Hollywood and viewed his job as a way to pay the bills. He made Bowery Boys films, and White Coaters like the infamous MOM & DAD, and ended his career with BILLY THE KID VS DRACULA

All this contextualizing (Oh no! I've turned an overcomplicated title card!) is a long way to say that BULLETFACE is not truly a Poverty Row picture, but I appreciate what Pyun was trying to do. Poverty Row films were shot on 35mm, were (mostly) in focus, and featured (mostly) audible sound. That's not the case with BULLETFACE. It was

funded independently to the tune of $100,000, shot on a 720p camera (low-end even at the time) and is technically compromised. The audio keeps cutting out. The video is fuzzy. Every scene is captured from one direction because Albert didn't have time to move the lights. The camera wobbles around unpleasantly throughout in an attempt to make things dynamic. You can clearly feel that Pyun shot BULLETFACE in a gruelling 5½ days. And while the best Poverty Row films were often simple to  a fault, BULLETFACE is unnecessarily complicated. It should be the straightforward story of a woman (Victoria Maurette) out for revenge, so why are there so many title cards? And a subplot about a drug harvested from woman's spines? And an abundance of grimy rape, torture, and nudity?

So, what's the difference between BULLETFACE and Pyun's previous three-day wonder DECEIT (1989)? DECEIT was shot on 35mm, in one location, and had a clear, straightforward story. DECEIT oozes confidence and style. BULLETFACE feels desperate. Pyun shot DECEIT right after he finished CYBORG. He was hungry, wanted to experiment, and had something to prove. BULLETFACE came at the tail end of a career where all of Pyun's hard work had received very little appreciation. There are only so many times he could finish a project by the skin of his teeth before it became the norm, not the exception. Pyun spent his entire professional life showing the world he could deliver something with nothing, but instead of rewarding him, the money men kept taking things away.

Martin Scorsese likes to say he would have loved to be employed during the factory filmmaking era of the '40s. Directors would go into work at a studio, be handed a project, and be expected to go off and make it. And once they finished it, they'd be given another, and another, and another, as long as they brought the projects in on time and on budget. The idea of being in constant motion is a romantic idea, but one I don't believe Scorsese could have pulled off due to his temperament.

Albert Pyun did it.

His career in the DTV trenches was the equivalent of the factory line studio era. He took the jobs, whatever they may be, and he delivered them on time and budget, and unlike journeymen like William Beaudine, Pyun succeeded in putting his stamp on the projects. Sometimes they were great (MEAN GUNS), sometimes they were off (HONG KONG '97), but his voice was always present.

It wasn't enough.

Unfortunately, Pyun rarely felt he succeeded. His films had their budgets cut, were re-edited without his consent or wholly misunderstood by the public. BULLETFACE is a project where Pyun had control. I'm not a fan of it, but it's still his, and I don't want to take that away from him. I'd rather see an artist do what they love, audience be damned, if it brings joy to their life. Especially if that artist is Albert Pyun.

FUN FACT Director Edgar G. Ulmer (DETOUR) is one of the few appreciated auteurs of the Poverty Row era, and his career trajectory is very similar to that of Pyun's. Ulmer worked in the big leagues early on with his Universal picture THE BLACK CAT (SWORD AND THE SORCERER), was kicked to skid row and made DETOUR (DECEIT), and had a brief brush with mainstream success again with RUTHLESS (ADRENALIN: FEAR THE RUSH). Eventually, Ulmer had to leave the states to work with washed up stars on foreign productions like HANNIBAL (CRAZY SIX) before he ended making minimalist projects like THE MAN FROM PLANET X (INVASION). The difference is that Ulmer's clear expressionist style can be effortlessly latched onto while Pyun's direct-to-video origins (all of Ulmer's films were released theatrically) and emphasis on the action genre make him more disreputable.

ABELAR: TALES OF AN ANCIENT EMPIRE (2010)

CAST
Inbar Lavi, Kevin Sorbo, Michael Paré

WRITER
Cynthia Curnan

PRODUCERS
Cynthia Curnan, Nicholas Celozzi

CINEMATOGRAPHER
Philip Alan Waters

MUSIC
Anthony Riparetti

PRODUCTION DESIGNER
James Terry Welden

EDITOR
David Lamb

COSTUME DESIGN
Glenda Maddox

RUNTIME
86 mins

BACK OF THE BOX Swords clash and destinies collide in this epic story of bloodlust and vengeance. Xia, a demonic sorceress, has sworn to destroy Queen Ma' at her kingdom of Abelar. As Xia and her army of vampires terrorize the land, the queen dispatches Princess Tanis to find the one man who can stop Xia — Oda (Michael Paré), a cold-blooded mercenary who is revealed to be Tanis' biological father. Joined by a thieving rogue named Aedan (Kevin Sorbo) Tanis begins a danger-filled quest that pits her against the sister she never knew — a half-human, half-vampire creature determined to kill Oda.

TALES OF AN ANCIENT EMPIRE is a mess. It was supposed to be a sequel to Pyun's first film THE SWORD AND THE SORCERER, but TALES had so many production issues that the final result ended up as a flimsy patchwork of scenes shuffled together seemingly at random. It should have been a pretty straightforward fantasy adventure (Vampire Queen. Heroes need to murder her. Etc.), and it looks like Pyun shot a chunk of the film as a conventional sword-and-sorcery picture, but then the money evaporated, and he was forced had to wrap up the project with nothing but a green screen.

The film opens with an overcomplicated introduction that features Michael Paré in a terrible wig for fifteen minutes, and then focuses on Kevin Sorbo as a charming rogue who gathers up a team of women mercenaries for fifty minutes, and then just as things are getting going, the film forgets about Sorbo for the rest of the picture and goes back to Michael Paré on a green screen. Instead of a proper climax, the audience is treated to a bunch of still frames accompanied with the narration, "And then the heroes defeated the villain!" Oh, and there are fifteen minutes of credits.

A production company signed off on this? And released it to the public? It's especially infuriating because the lengthy middle section of TALES is actually fun. All the characters crack wise, there's some clever physical stuff, and there are even a few horses! Cheap on-location work is always better than a digital backlot.

On the bright side, the film did reunite a gaggle of people that had worked with Pyun in the past: Olivier Gruner, Sasha Mitchell, Ralf Moeller, Norbert Weisser, Scott Paulin, Xavier Declie, Michael Paré, Victoria Maurette, and Morgan Weisser all make brief green screen assisted appearances. Even actor Lee Horsely (the star of SWORD AND THE SORCERER) shows up for a hot second, which is surprising, considering he and Pyun famously had a problematic experience the first time around. TALES was shot by Philip Alan Waters (CAPTAIN AMERICA), scored by Anthony Riparetti, and even George Mooradian, Pyun's cinematographer from the golden period, showed up on set to help out for a few days. It feels like a farewell to the film family Pyun had built up over his impressive 28-year career.

FUN FACT The film may be nothing but a sad curio, but the DVD released by E1 has an interesting special feature: 40 minutes of behind the scenes footage from the green screen portion of the shoot. I can't recall seeing any other substantial video evidence of Albert on set, so it's an essential document of his working method. The cast of Pyun veterans and new recruits all get interviewed, and while they are very polite in their praise of the man's work, it's obvious most of them haven't seen his last few films. There's an interview with Sasha Mitchell where he goes "He's great with action" followed by a cut to Mitchell pathetically wrestling with a vampire in front of a green screen.

SLINGER (1989/2013)

CAST
Jean-Claude Van Damme, Deborah Richter, Vincent Klyn

WRITER
Albert Pyun (as Kitty Chalmers)

PRODUCERS
Yoram Globus, Menahem Golan

CINEMATOGRAPHER
Philip Alan Waters

MUSIC
Anthony Riparetti, James Saad

PRODUCTION DESIGNER
Douglas H. Leonard

EDITORS
Scott Stevenson, Rozanne Zingale

COSTUME DESIGN
Heidi Kaczenski

RUNTIME
82 mins

BACK OF THE BOX Albert Pyun presents his original 1989 Director's Cut entitled "SLINGER". Available for the first time.

THE DIRECTOR'S CUT OF CYBORG is all about an extreme shift in tone. The theatrical release is an '80s post-apocalyptic actioner about delivering a cure to save the world. It's colourful, wooden, and goofy. The Director's Cut is a hopeless road movie where the heroes are hunted down by a group of Satan worshippers. The structure is the same in both, but in Pyun's original vision, there's a sense of despair to it all. The most significant difference is the radically different score by Jim Saad and Tony Riparetti. The release version of CYBORG features a chintzy midi number written by a journeyman composer. The original score is sludge rock epic built on groaning guitars and hair raising feedback.

Pyun showed his first cut to Cannon executives with the sound turned up to 11. The bigwigs left complaining of headaches. He begged them to let him release it in black and white. They told him they'd rather shoot themselves in the head. After a public preview proved to be a disaster, JCVD stepped in and re-cut the film. The released version would cement the public perception of Albert Pyun as a hack sci-fi director.

I don't blame the audience's adverse reaction to Pyun's vision. His Director's Cut of CYBORG is miserable in the most artful of ways. It's grim, mean and forceful. The original version always left me bewildered because JCVD came off as such a weenie. Why didn't he fight until half an hour in? Why did he always run away from danger? Why did he constantly get beaten up? (Okay, I liked that part.) It only became apparent when watching the Director's Cut that all those elements were conscious choices in Pyun's conception of the film. JCVD is the disgraced samurai, a loser who only jumps into action when he has no other choice. In the DC, every fight scene is coloured with pure desperation.

The villain Fender (Vincent Klyn) is a silent brute in the Theatrical Version, but in the DC, he's a Chatty Cathy who is continuously praising the lord of darkness and mocking Van Damme's attempts at fighting back. It's a little much (less is more), but you get a clearer  image of Pyun's thematic goal: The hollow value of revenge - which would have been a perfectly fine subject to tackle in a European art film about WWII, but studio executives were horrified to find Pyun had inserted it into a picture that starred a guy who built his fame on doing the splits.

At his best, Pyun pushed against the confines of every genre he worked in. The problem was that he wasn't very diplomatic about it. His choices always ran up against the iron-clad expectations of a picture's intended audience. He didn't just want to do something different; he wanted to rattle the viewer and turn their world upside down. You expected ADRENALIN: FEAR THE RUSH to be a lightweight Christopher Lambert romp? Nope! You get a relentlessly downbeat nightmare trip with no heroes. Do you want a pulpy CAPTAIN AMERICA adventure? Too bad! He's a loser, and the American dream is a lie. How about a fun post-apocalyptic action film starring the guy that busts a move in BREAKIN? Sorry! Pyun is going to slap you in the face with the end of the world.

If there's one thing I hope you've gleaned from all this, it's that Albert Pyun always tried his best to do something different. Did it always work? Hell no. Most of the time, it failed miserably due to a lack of focus, a boatload of impossible goals, and a system that would never accept his experiments.

But goddammit, he tried.

SAD FACT There isn't any "proper" version of the Director's Cut of CYBORG. Pyun released his workprint on DVD, but even that version is missing a lot of violence that he was forced to snip out, and the fuzzy video and muffled audio quality make it a tough watch. In Germany, Digidreams Studios put out a Blu-ray in which they did their best to mix the VHS workprint with a remastered cut of the theatrical release. The result is better, but still lacking in several ways. The most annoying element is that every extended shot is crossfaded between both versions to keep the picture in sync, which is very jarring when it happens every few seconds. Still, it's probably the best we'll ever get. For some reason, neither Albert nor Digidreams have offered the film in black and white, so pop in the Director's Cut and set the saturation on your television/video player to 0. Trust me. It makes all the difference. In black and white, Pyun's artful compositions gain a whole other level of expressionist grandeur

THE INTERROGATION OF CHERYL COOPER (2014)

CAST
Shane Ryan, Tommie Vegas, Brittany Bochart

WRITER
Cynthia Curnan

PRODUCERS
Cynthia Curnan, Tony Riparetti, Michael Su

CINEMATOGRAPHER
Michael Su

MUSIC
Anthony Riparetti

PRODUCTION DESIGNER
(Uncredited)

EDITOR
Chiba & Nobu
(Albert Pyun's Dogs)

COSTUME DESIGN
(Uncredited)

RUNTIME
70 mins

BACK OF THE BOX A young woman Cheryl Cooper (Tommie Vegas) awakens in handcuffs and in a room alone. As she regains her senses we can see she is covered in blood. Shortly a man enters the room. He says he is Detective Ben (Shane Ryan) and tells Cheryl she was the only survivor of a horrific mass murder at a closed and abandoned resort in Las Vegas Nevada. The Detective commences to interrogate Cheryl and events soon do not seem as the Detective or Cheryl claim leading to an unexpected and shocking climax.

WHAT'S THE SIMPLEST THING A FILMMAKER CAN DO?

Albert Pyun's last released film is a stage play shot in one long take.

It takes place in a bare room with a table in the center. Two characters sit across from each other. Cheryl (Tommie Vegas) has her hands tied behind her back. She stares through mascara-drenched eyes at her interrogator Detective Ben (Shane Ryan). Cheryl just survived a brutal massacre that killed her friends. Ben questions her about it. The camera moves from left to right. Shakily. Sometimes it zooms in. The conversation isn't very illuminating. It falls into a repetitive rhythm. Tommie Vegas gives a pretty compelling performance as the shell-shocked Cheryl, but she doesn't have much to do.

At one point, Cheryl and Detective Ben turn toward the camera, and some static appears over the screen to imply they're looking at a security cam footage from the massacre. They describe what they're seeing, but the viewer doesn't get to witness it. We learn Ben is the killer. Or is he? I believe some title cards seem to indicate Cheryl may be the murderer? And to complicate things even further, an more text implies Cheryl is the same

character from Pyun's found-footage film INVASION. The characters mention meteors, but I couldn't grasp how it all intersected. Is she supposed to be crazy because she was infected by the aliens? Or was it all in her mind? Either way, it's at once too simple in its presentation and way over-complicated in its conclusions.

THE INTERROGATION FOR CHERYL COOPER exists for one reason only: Albert Pyun has to make movies. And at this point, it's not for any commercial purposes. He just needs to do it because it's what he does.

PERSONAL ASIDE CHERYL screened at the Pollygrind Film Festival in Las Vegas the same year my first feature film TEDDY BOMB premiered there. It was the first time anything I made was going to play to a large audience, and I was thrilled to learn that Pyun would be attending as well. It was especially serendipitous because TEDDY BOMB is filled with references to NEMESIS: someone quotes Tim Thomerson's villain, a cyborg makes an appearance, and I sneaked in a close-up of the cover of NEMESIS. It was a match made in heaven! Well, that was until the organizer announced the festival was having financial troubles and was going to have to be cancelled. I was crushed. We had already bought the plane tickets!

Miraculously, Albert swooped in and saved the day by renting a gigantic theatre out to accommodate my screening - and it wasn't even on the night his film was playing! He just wanted to make sure none of the other filmmakers were disappointed. I ended up watching TEDDY BOMB on a massive screen in recliner seats. Sadly, due to health issues, Albert was not able to attend the opening night of the festival. I wish I could have shaken his hand in person and thanked him for his kind act. It meant the world to me.

INTERVIEW
TONY RIPARETTI
(COMPOSER/SOUND DESIGNER)

How did you get started in the music industry?

Like most kids back in the day, it was when I saw the Beatles on the Ed Sullivan Show and thought "Oh I have to do that." I had been listening to music before, but not as intently until then, and I was in a band, but we were doing other people's songs, and then we started writing our own stuff.

Did you ever imagine that you'd end up working in film as a composer?

I loved cinema growing up, but I never thought I'd make music in the industry. At that time, I wasn't a schooled player, and I didn't do any orchestral dates or anything like that, but I was with Sue and Jim in the band SUE SAAD AND THE NEXT in L.A. Jim was credited as James Lance in the group because he didn't want anyone to know he was married to Sue because at the time it wasn't very Rock 'N Roll! I had met Jim when I was 12, Sue joined the band when I was 15, so we had been together for a long time before we met Albert. The story goes there was a film music supervisor on RADIOACTIVE DREAMS, and she got him a tape of what we were doing, so he called us. He asked us if we scored any films and we said "Yeah! We've done that!" and he figured out we hadn't but brought us on anyway. We started slow, did a couple of cues, a couple of songs, and he even put Sue in the film. I thought "This is kind of cool. I could make a living and not have to go on tour."

You weren't attracted to the tour life?

We did a few smaller tours that I did enjoy, but I did miss being in the studio. So, when I met a woman, and she had two little ones, I went, "Oh, I can't go on the road now." And I was happy to be working in film.

You wrote a lot of songs in VICIOUS LIPS (1986). It was basically a musical!

So many! We had five songs in there. That was good, and the songs were fun to do, but it took a while. There was a girl in the film miming what Sue sang, and the actor did a really good job doing it! Most of the time, it looks totally off.

Do you know why a soundtrack was never released?

We never did a soundtrack because the film just disappeared. It got put in storage someplace. It was lost for many years. Me and Albert looked around the world for it. And then suddenly, it came out.

Yeah, it was put on Blu-ray a few years ago.

It was nice to see it have a second life.

I read there were a lot of problems on the production.

Albert didn't really talk to us about that stuff. I think he put it all in a different compartment. We were always in the studio working. I did a lot of films with him, and I've visited the set maybe five times over the years.

At what point would he involve you in the process?

He would usually call us up when I was working on one, and he'd be starting another. Jim and I were never on the sets because we were always scoring while Albert was off shooting a different film. I found out about the problems later on when Albert and I started doing it all ourselves. At that time, I learned it's crazy to make money doing movies, but before then, he left me out of it so I wouldn't worry and could complete the job.

What was the story behind your rejected score for CYBORG (1986)? I love that score. It makes the film feel completely different.

Jim and I worked so hard on that. It was our first big electric score, so many guitars, distorted drums, and we just went in and said, "We'll just do what we do. This is how we jam!" We got into that space and spent a lot of time on it. We really liked what we did and were so disappointed that it wasn't in the final film. We got replaced by another composer. It's not his fault, but for us, that was a career-changing experience right there. That was one of Albert's big projects, and we were out of it. I believe we would have been pushed up if our score had come out at the time, but you can't cry too hard about that kind of stuff.

How did you and Jim Saad part ways as composers?

At the time, I was living in L.A., and he moved back up to Santa Barbara. We were splitting the scores, and he asked Albert for more money, and Albert told him, "Sorry, but no," so Jim went "Alright. Then I have to stop."

Were you able to live off the income of your scoring work?

I always had a recording studio, but I could live off the score work. I also made money on residuals when the films played on HBO and such, but now with streaming, I don't get anything. I get a cheque for like, eight cents. The composers are unprotected and unrecognized. We're the red headed step-children of the industry. We're still one of the few components of film that doesn't have a union.

Would Albert give you any direction to guide your scores?

In the very beginning, he would say, "Come down to the edit," and he'd show me a few rough scenes. Then he'd say "Follow me," and we'd go out to his Volvo sedan, and he'd open the trunk, and there'd be hundreds of cassettes. He'd start throwing them at me and go "Listen to this… and this… and listen to this!" So I knew what realm he wanted me in. I feel like all directors should do that, know what the feel of the film is like. Once people started doing temp, the temp music was the killer of creativity.

Back in the day, a composer would be trying to put a stamp on a film, and then it changed to trying to mimic someone else's temp score in a way where you hoped nobody would notice. Albert always let me have my say. We may not have always agreed on it, but it was better, even when we battled it out. Sometimes I would win, sometimes he would win, and sometimes we'd compromise. I didn't mind it, even when it got tough, because I felt really strongly about stuff like "What emotion am I bringing out?" Albert cared about the music. Some of the other directors didn't understand it, and it made them really tough to work with.

Do you remember any particular fights with Albert about a score?

It was mostly trying to be big enough for Albert. You're always running up against the gear that you have. When we started off, we didn't have enough money to sync to the film, so we had to wild sync, and that's why there are three composers — one guy is playing, one guy's pushing play, and the other is on the other instruments. People don't realize how hard it was to do because this newer generation has it so much easier. No tape!

My battles with Albert were all about the sonic element. How big can you make a MIDI score? There's only a certain amount of instruments you can put in before it sounds smaller and smaller. Like when you do a pseudo-orchestral score and the instruments aren't that great, and you're trying to make it sound big without having the bodies to perform in the studio.

My favourite thing was he'd always hear the score over the telephone and go "Tony! There's no bass! Where's the low end?" And I'd go, "Albert! There's no bass on a telephone!" I could never figure that one out with Albert. It happened every time. He'd come over to my place, hear it and go, "Oh, okay!" It was low budget, and it was hard for me to get all the gear and samplers that were better. I had to meander my way through it all. I'd get one new toy for each new film, and that's how I built it up. I still do that today. You get a movie, you gotta get a new toy to make the job easier.

Even during my last score for Albert, INTERSTELLAR CIVIL WAR, we battled over the songs for that. I was happy to sign my name on it. No hesitation! And he disagreed with me on some of the pieces. I did seven or eight songs on it. He always wanted women to sing on his stuff, and I said: "Albert, I've done this a long time, let me do sing for once!" But I don't know where it's at. I haven't spoken to him in a while.

When Albert came to you and said: "I want you to do ARCADE, BRAINSMASHER, and KICKBOXER 2..." how did you keep each score fresh in your mind?

Well, I didn't have many tools to work with, but I think the scores are different enough. They're all electronic, but they all come from different places. The one I had the most fun with was MEAN GUNS.

I love the MEAN GUNS score!

I got to bring in Mambo players and let the music got to go all over the place. I had a great time doing that score.

What was your reaction when Albert told you. "All Mambo. All the time."?

I went, "Really? Ooooohkay." Then I read the script and got it. "Ah, this is a black comedy! The music is offsetting the violence, light tunes over people kicking the crap out of each other." The film came out and then Mambo was all over the place. It was one of those things that Albert did before anyone else!

Did you ever get a sense of how the films were being received?

They were always killed by the reviewers. I didn't really want to read those. I think the most reviewers at the time thought he was schlocky, but he did a lot with very little money and very little time, and I don't think there are many directors who could do that. It was only later that people came back and realized what Albert did. Well, they've realized that overseas at least.

How fast did you have to work? Were the producers ever like "Hurry up! Or we'll recycle your cues from a previous film!"

I was nervous on every project because I was pushing the score up a mountain and going "I'm not going to finish it in time!" The scariest one was the orchestral score of POSTMORTEM.

How did that come about?

Albert was filming in Bratislava, I think he had just shot ADRENALIN, and there's an orchestra there at the Bratislava Radio Hall that did classical pieces, and we got a chance to use them for cheap.

I think I had four weeks, and I had never done it before, so I needed help. I wrote the music, but I couldn't do all the orchestration. I could go "This is what I hear for the clarinet," and they'd respond with "The clarinet can't actually go that high." The keyboard goes WAAAAY up here, but I didn't know the ranges of the other instruments. They could figure that out, and I learned that wasn't too big a problem. One problem was writing it all out for a 74 piece orchestra that recorded it in three days. That was tough. The hall where we recorded was one of the last buildings the Russians built - an upside down pyramid with a bunch of office buildings above. Underneath that point, there's an 1,800 seat auditorium. Beautiful. I was in the control room. There was a Bratislavan conductor and the engineers were tough. I kept wanting more string and they would go, "Not possible. This is the way that it is." They had much more power than they'd have in the states. These guys had probably recorded a lot of orchestration, and I could see why they would do it that way, but I just wanted the strings bigger in my mix! At the time, we only got stereo mixes from it, straight to DAT machines. But in the end, it turned out good. I would love to have another shot at an orchestral score. We did it for cheap. At the time, they were still green at doing film scores, and they weren't quite used to it. I had a song in the movie that's a 6/8 kind of thing, but it had to have an Irish lilt to it, and while I know they'd be able to do it now, at the time they didn't understand what I was trying to do. Honestly, I may not have been written out correctly. I was pretty spent after those few days. Everyone else got to stay and visit, and I had to come back because they needed the score put in the film immediately. Now, I listen to it, and I'm a lot less critical than when I first did it.

Has Albert ever told you "The score is going to be the backbone of the film"? I'm thinking of CRAZY SIX (1997) where the music never stops.

A lot of the times it would be that way. I don't really like doing that, but Albert demanded it. To me, it sometimes made the music less than what it was because there was so much of it.

BLAST (1997) has that feel too.

I think I got pretty good at doing it, but it was never my first choice. I think a lot of the time Albert was afraid to just let the scene play. He would get good actors, and I'd wonder, "Why not just let them do their thing?" If there was no music on the later films, he'd add in sound design, because he didn't want anything to sit there. I was like, "Albert! Just let it breathe a little!" But he was relentless, it's the way he filmed, it's the way he edited, always relentless.

Do you remember how some of the music from RADIOACTIVE DREAMS ended up in SPITFIRE (1995)?

That was all Albert. He said, "You own it? Let's do it!" I never minded that. I've heard Hans Zimmer, who I love, use alt cues in a lot of his movies. When I was working on two films at once, I'd be like "Yeah, go ahead, no problem!" On the '90s films, I sometimes worked on two of his films at once, and I didn't like that. I'd say, "What am I working on again? Why does this sound so familiar?" Because you're trying to switch back and forth. Not my favourite cup of tea. Albert would shoot a film like BULLETFACE (2010), and he would cue it with a lot of my old scores and say, "I like this!" And I'd say, "Go ahead!" He'd sometimes use footage from his films in later projects, like shots where there weren't any actors in it.

Did you ever think the work with Albert was going to slow down?

You look ahead and go "At some point, it'll happen," but I was known as the guy who worked with Albert and I never really went to pound the pavement to get other scores, because Albert kept me working for 34 years. It's my fault because I didn't push things hard enough, so I didn't make a lot of those connections. I never met anybody! I was always working in the studio trying to get the scores done much to the chagrin of my wife and kids.

Did you get many offers from people other than Albert to score films?

I did do scores for other companies, small films, but not until Albert took a break to take care of his dad, and then there were a couple of years where we weren't working together.

How did you get into the sound design side of things?

A lot of the time in the early '90s, I didn't hear any of the sound design until the mix! Like in NEMESIS 2, 3, 4 I created the sounds for things in my score, but it ended up half a second apart, so it would sound so out of tune with the sound design. Those guys were a whole different crew. I've been in Santa Barbara since '96, so that also made it easier for me to do it. I said, "I don't want to go down to L.A. anymore," so Albert said, "Do you want to do the sound design?" And I went "Uhhhhh...Yeah?" I didn't know what I was getting into. I like it, but it takes a long time.

Albert and I were partners by the end. He did all the filming, and I would do all the sound. I like working like that with him now, but it was a lot of work for one guy on my end of things. But you know what's so cool about that? It's interesting to go "I'm building the film on the sonic side." It's a creative process for me to start with poorly recorded dialogue and make it all work.

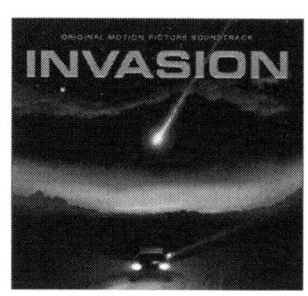

What were some of your favourite films to work on as a sound designer?

INFECTION (AKA INVASION) was a really fun one to do. We went to Lionsgate, Albert and me, to play INFECTION (2005) for the big wigs. We even set up to their room to play in 5.1 because it could only do stereo. As they watched, we went to the commissary, and eventually, they all came out saying, "Oh my god, we were so afraid!"

The film is very much a roller coaster ride.

It is! Now, it doesn't quite feel as fresh today, but at the time it was very forward thinking, and Lionsgate got it! But the people who did the marketing didn't get it at all. The film wasn't portrayed in the right way. It's a shame because the suits couldn't stop gabbing away about it. Usually, people are like "You're fired! Get out of here!". Unfortunately, the outcome for INFECTION was still the same. They dumped it. Did you ever get to see LEFT FOR DEAD?

Oh yeah! Your score and sound design for LEFT FOR DEAD (2007) are amazing.

I appreciate that! It was a lengthy endeavour that took almost six years to do, with a couple of years in between, as we waited for the software to catch up with the problems we had. That film left me for dead because we worked on it for so long. Albert once said he did 300 versions of it... and I believe him! I didn't do all of them, but I worked on a lot and was like "Albert stop! Please! Stop!" In the end, I did like what he did. I was happy and bummed that it never got out there more.

Were there any scores you thought would breakthrough?

I always thought we'd go theatrical. It always surprised me when we went straight to video. I only found out about that after the film was done. It would always start as a theatrical release and "This is going to be very good." I mean, every filmmaker does that. We're going to try our hardest before we put it out there. That has never stopped. I have felt the same way with the last films I did with Albert. They deserve to be out there, but it isn't even straight to video anymore. It's straight to streaming, and there's no money in it. We had problems with INFECTION because it was stolen.

It was pirated online?

Yeah, someone leaked it, and that means your film is worth nothing, even if a distributor picked it up. Those things were tough. MEAN GUNS was killed when it was released. A company bought the film, then they went bankrupt, and we brought them to court, but I haven't seen a dime from that. I have so many songs and music that I haven't made any money on. Albert would say, "Go to Europe and get lawyers!" and I just couldn't imagine making a dent in those big corporations. We've had some bad luck with that stuff, but it's really the nature of the business.

Did you ever get the sense that the films were being taken out of Albert's hands?

Yes. It wasn't good. They would change the video, but they never fixed the audio!

I'd love to go in and change some of the things I worked for years on they screwed up at the last minute. Even the Lionsgate releases. They're a giant company! They have the stems! Why couldn't they do it right? And Albert likes to change things too. He'd say, "This is the final version," and I'd hand it all over, but then I'd look at it afterwards, and he would have moved things around.

You're credited as an executive producer on TALES OF AN ANCIENT EMPIRE (2010). Were you more involved in the production side of things on the later films?

Not really. I'm an executive producer on a lot of stuff! Albert just gave that title to help me out. I was never involved in the production.

Has a record company ever asked you to put any of your scores out on vinyl? I don't believe any of your film music has ever been released in that format.

There are a couple of score CDs on Howling Wolf records, but no one has ever asked me about vinyl releases. The problem is that in the '90s I was recording onto Tascam digital tapes and I lost all those scores because those tapes went bad after 10 years. I lost all my music going way back. Thankfully, I printed the 16 track mixes do a DAT recorder, but now I'm stuck with that, and the DAT versions weren't meant to be listened too without the movie. I keep thinking, "Ah if I had the 16 track version, I would do such a different mix!" This is reminding me I have more scores I have to digitize! As far as going vinyl goes, I don't know, I've never really thought about it.

Have you ever thought of going back to composing film scores?

I'd love to do more films! I'd love to do another one with Albert. I don't want to wind down. I feel more creative than I ever have right now, but the problem with me is that going down to L.A. is tough. I have a lot of experience, and I have my own studio, but the last time I spoke to my old agent they wanted to put me on the HOME NETWORK show, and I went "Naw, I'd rather go surfing."

THE PYUN PLAYERS

Albert Pyun loved to surround himself with familiar faces on projects and I've done my best to highlight the major players below.

For the sake of brevity, I've limited my selection to people who have appeared four or more times in Pyun productions, because it would otherwise stretch on forever due to the fact that he regularly shot films back to back and often re-used whoever was around.

THE ACTORS

Deborah Van Valkenburgh (4): A spunky ass kicker best remembered for her roles in Walter Hill's THE WARRIORS, Van Valkenburgh would appear in Pyun's filmography as Teri Hatcher's sister (BRAINSMASHER), a criminal (MEAN GUNS) and her character from STREETS OF FIRE in Pyun's pseudo-sequel ROAD TO HELL.

Andrew Divoff (4): Most famous for portraying the lead villain in WISHMASTER, Divoff showed up as an authority figure in the slickest of Pyun productions (BLAST) as well as the cheapest of the cheap (NEMESIS 4: DEATH ANGEL)

Brion James (4): Best known for going to toe to toe with Harrison Ford in BLADE RUNNER, Brion James was one of the great menacing character actors, but he mostly played villainous sidekicks with a goofy accents in Pyun films like NEMESIS and SPITFIRE.

Christian Andrews (6): There isn't much information I could find about Christian Andrews, but I assume he was a friend of Albert because he played the first Brick Bardo in RADIOACTIVE DREAMS, donned a creature suit for VICIOUS LIPS and took part in DECEIT and BLOODMATCH.

Yuji Okomoto (6): A charismatic performer who played the villain in KARATE KID 2, Pyun cast him as a slick killer (NEMESIS), a shaolin monk (BRAINSMASHER), and Thom Mathew's assassin buddy (MEAN GUNS).

Michael Hasley (7): A lanky British actor who always commanded the screen, Halsey played a goon (DOLLMAN), a detective (POSTMORTEM) and an Irish terrorist (TICKET) under Pyun's direction.

Scott Paulin (7): Brought into Pyun's world by his good friend Norbert Weisser for DECEIT, Paulin would go on to portray the Red Skull under a layer of painful makeup in CAPTAIN AMERICA, appear in KNIGHTS, and then return for a number of pictures during Pyun's freedom period (BULLETFACE).

Jahi J.J. Zuri (9): A first generation student of Bruce Lee, Zuri appeared in quite a few Pyun productions, but unfortunately never really got a chance to properly display his skill set in films like NEMESIS 2 and BLAST. His most prominent role was in OMEGA DOOM where he appeared as Rutger Hauer's first opponent.

Nicholas Guest (9): An all purpose actor who could do everything under the sun (He made his career as a voice actor), Guest is a chameleon in most of his Pyun film appearances, and they ran the gamut from wisecracking robot fighter (KNIGHTS) to a slick goon (NEMESIS).

Tina Cote (9): For a stretch in the mid 90s, Tina was all over Pyun's work as a killer cyborg (OMEGA DOOM), a ditzy moll (MEAN GUNS) and a martial arts coach (HEATSEEKER). Like a lot of the repertoire performers during this period, her last role was in the unfinished green screen film SORCERERS.

Tim Thomerson (10): A grizzled looking leading man with an aptitude for well timed wise-cracks, Tim Thomerson only starred in one Pyun film (DOLLMAN), but also played a dastardly villain (NEMESIS), an agent of the law (BRAINSMASHER), a dopey sidekick (SPITFIRE) and so much more.

Thom Mathews (12): A member of the horror hall of fame for starring in RETURN OF THE LIVING DEAD and in FRIDAY THE 13TH PART SIX: JASON LIVES, Mathews was Pyun's good luck charm. He was the teen bully with a conscience (DANGEROUSLY CLOSE), the man with a gun in his face (NEMESIS) and a psycho assassin (MEAN GUNS). His only starring role for Pyun was in the quickie martial arts revenge picture BLOODMATCH.

Vincent Klyn (14): A surfer who accompanied a friend to an audition for Pyun's unmade MASTERS OF THE UNIVERSE 2 and scored the role of CYBORG's villainous Fender in the process. He was Pyun's go-to guy to get in a scuffle with the hero, which he did in BLOODMATCH, RAVEN HAWK and BLAST.

Norbert Weisser (19): The king of Pyun Players, Norbert would do everything that Pyun offered without batting an eye. His roles include a mad scientist (ARCADE), Dennis Hopper's tattooed sidekick (TICKER) and a decapitated head. (OMEGA DOOM)

THE CREW

Cynthia Curnan (8): She was first credited as the screenwriter of the unreleased SORCERERS (1998), but from INVASION (2005) onward Curnan would write, produce and perform hundreds of miscellaneous tasks on every subsequent film. Cynthia and Albert are happily married in Las Vegas.

Philip Alan Waters (11): A cinematographer that gave Pyun's early films like CYBORG, DECEIT, and CAPTAIN AMERICA a slick and colourful comic book feel. Waters and Pyun would part ways for most of the '90s, but would get back together for the URBAN trilogy and have continued to collaborate since then.

Ken Morrisey (15): An editor who worked with Albert from HONG KONG '97 (1994) till BULLETFACE (2010). He didn't edit every picture during that time, Natasha Gjurokovic did three films starting with BLAST, but he'd always come back to collaborate with Pyun and the gang.

Gary Schmoeller (18): From 1994 onwards Gary Schmoeller would be involved as a producer on Pyun's films until BULLETFACE (2010). He helped produce a number of Brian Yuzna films (SOCIETY) and made his career working as an "indie producer" with the company Filmwerks.

George Mooradian (24): From KICKBOXER 2 (1991) onward, Mooradian was the cinematographer integral to defining the look of Pyun's golden period. Their last major collaboration was POSTMORTEM (1999) after which Mooradian went on to work regularly with Director Louis Morneau (RETROACTIVE) before transitioning to sitcoms like ACCORDING TO JIM which resulted in five daytime Emmy nominations.

Tom Karnowski (29): I know he's a producer who was an essential part of all of Pyun's major productions, but I couldn't find much background information about him. All I know is that he and Pyun were childhood friends in Hawaii, he co-wrote THE SWORD AND THE SORCERER and came to Hollywood with Pyun to produce it. He jumped between the roles of Producer, Line Producer, and First Assistant Director on all of Pyun's productions right up till the URBAN trilogy. Pyun speaks fondly of him on his commentary tracks and says things like "The production would have stopped dead on some days if Tom didn't show up with a briefcase full of money to pay the cast and crew." Karnowski would go on to produce a number of big Hollywood productions like Emmerich's 10,000 BC (2008), Spielberg's THE POST (2017) and a number of films with Write/Director Rian Johnson which includes STAR WARS: THE LAST JEDI (2017).

EPILOGUE

> "All I ever wanted to do was make a feature film and have it play at the Waikiki 2, which was my favourite theater growing up in Hawaii. I achieved that with my first film, and so, everything since 1982 has been gravy."
>
> — Albert Pyun

On August 19th 2013, Albert Pyun announced on Facebook that he was retiring from filmmaking due to health issues that included constant pain, dementia, and heart problems.

His retirement did not last long.

As of this writing, Albert Pyun's IMDB lists that he's since completed a film (INTERSTELLAR CIVIL WAR: SHADOWS OF THE EMPIRE), is in production on another (BADASS ANGELS AND DEMONS) and currently has three more on the horizon (CYBORG NEMESIS: THE DARK RIFT, THE KICKBOXER: ALGIERS, and CITY OF BLOOD).

He will never stop.

He's a filmmaker after all.

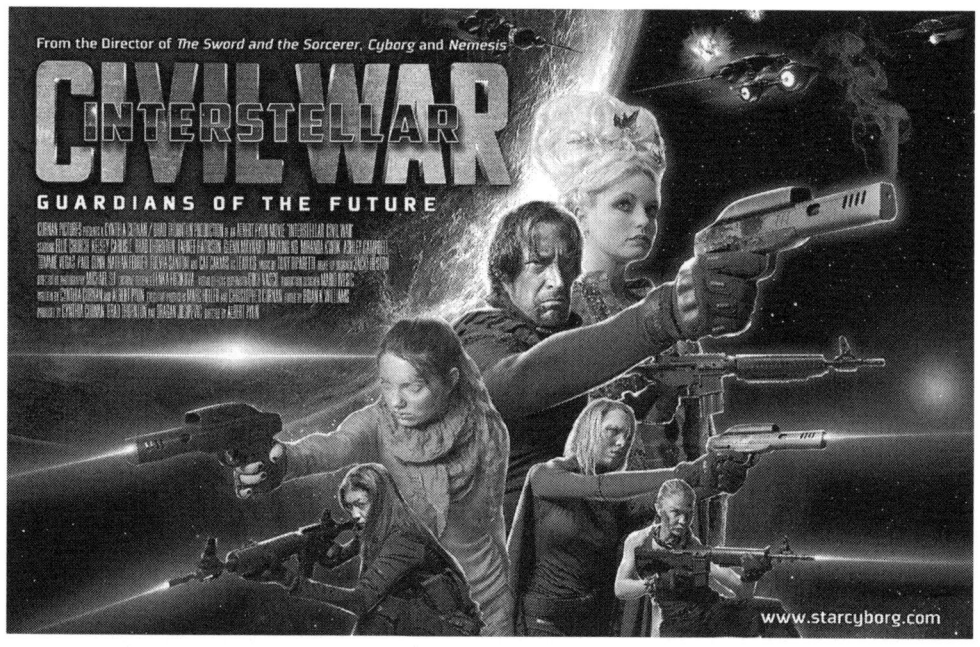

BIBLIOGRAPHY

Cult People: Tales from Hollywood's Exploitation A-list
Loreti - Headpress - 2010

The Good, The Tough & The Deadly: Action Movies & Stars, 1960s-present
Moore - Schiffer Publishing Ltd. - 2016

World Gone Wild: A Survivor's Guide to Post-Apocalyptic Movies
Moore & Vern - Schiffer Publishing Ltd. - 2014

IT CAME FROM THE VIDEO AISLE!: Inside Charles Band's Full Moon Entertainment Studio
Jay et al. - Schiffer Publishing Ltd.- 2017

Empire of the 'b's: the mad movie world of Charles Band
Jay et al. - Hemlock Books Limited - 2014'

Seagalogy: a study of the ass-kicking films of Steven Seagal
Vern - Titan - 2012

SPECIAL THANKS

Emily Milling (for listening to me talk about this endlessly and laying it all out)

Will Sloan (for reading it over)

Keenan Marr Tamblyn (for making the classic style posters)

Duncan Bruce (for illustrating The Periods of Pyun)

Andrew Barr (for creating the cover)

Adam 'The Riot' Thorn (for showing me NEMESIS)

Peter Kuplowsky (for helping me watch NEMESIS twice in a theatre)

Mathew Kumar (for falling in love with RADIOACTIVE DREAMS with me in Austin)

Norbert Weisser, George Mooradian and Tony Riparetti (for all your hard work and taking the time to speak to me)

and

Albert Pyun (for making all those movies and never giving up)

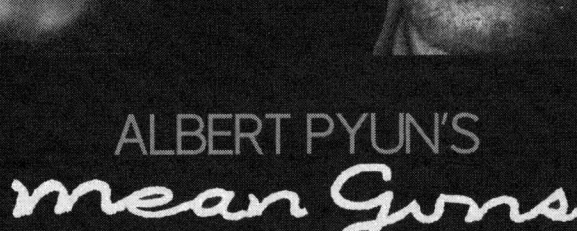